Unhooking from Whiteness

CONSTRUCTING KNOWLEDGE: CURRICULUM STUDIES IN ACTION

Volume 6

Scope

"Curriculum" is an expansive term; it encompasses vast aspects of teaching and learning. Curriculum can be defined as broadly as, "The content of schooling in all its forms" (English, p. 4), and as narrowly as a lesson plan. Complicating matters is the fact that curricula are often organized to fit particular time frames. The incompatible and overlapping notions that curriculum involves everything that is taught and learned in a particular setting *and* that this learning occurs in a limited time frame reveal the nuanced complexities of curriculum studies.

"Constructing Knowledge" provides a forum for systematic reflection on the substance (subject matter, courses, programs of study), purposes, and practices used for bringing about learning in educational settings. Of concern are such fundamental issues as: What should be studied? Why? By whom? In what ways? And in what settings? Reflection upon such issues involves an inter-play among the major components of education: subject matter, learning, teaching, and the larger social, political, and economic contexts, as well as the immediate instructional situation. Historical and autobiographical analyses are central in understanding the contemporary realties of schooling and envisioning how to (re)shape schools to meet the intellectual and social needs of all societal members. Curriculum is a social construction that results from a set of decisions; it is written and enacted and both facets undergo constant change as contexts evolve.

This series aims to extent the professional conversation about curriculum in contemporary educational settings. Curriculum is a designed experience intended to promote learning. Because it is socially constructed, curriculum is subject to all the pressures and complications of the diverse communities that comprise schools and other social contexts in which citizens gain self-understanding.

Unhooking from Whiteness

The Key to Dismantling Racism in the United States

Edited by

Cleveland Hayes
University of Laverne, USA

and

Nicholas D. Hartlep
Illinois State University, USA

SENSE PUBLISHERS
ROTTERDAM/BOSTON/TAIPEI

A C.I.P. record for this book is available from the Library of Congress.

ISBN: 978-94-6209-375-1 (paperback)
ISBN: 978-94-6209-376-8 (hardback)
ISBN: 978-94-6209-377-5 (e-book)

Published by: Sense Publishers,
P.O. Box 21858,
3001 AW Rotterdam,
The Netherlands
https://www.sensepublishers.com/

Printed on acid-free paper

Cover design by Tak Toyoshima

TABLE OF CONTENTS

TABLE OF CONTENTS

vi

ACKNOWLEDGMENTS

Cleveland would like to thank all of the contributors to this project; if it were not for their willingness to open themselves up, this project would not have become what it became. A special thanks to the reviewers Paul Gorski and Warren Blumenfeld, and to Rema Reynolds and Joy Lei for adding their perspectives to this project. Cleveland would also like to especially thank Brenda Juárez, Darron Smith, and Audrey Thompson for exposing him to Whiteness Theory. He thanks his colleagues in Advanced Studies in Education and other important influences in the College of Education and Organizational Leadership. Lastly, a special thanks to Joseph Kelly for everything he has done behind the scenes to make this work possible, and to Robin Saunders for taking care of Sadie when he is away presenting this work. He also wants to dedicate this book to his grandmother Olivia Durr Hayes Smith August 16, 1918–May 21, 2012.

Nicholas would like to thank Paul Gorski, Warren Blumenfeld, and Nicholas Ozment; Gorski and Blumenfeld for their insightful feedback on chapters presented in this book, and Ozment for his copyediting expertise. Nicholas would also like to thank Cleveland Hayes for his thoughtfulness when conceptualizing such a book. This book originated because of some wonderful discussions at the American Educational Research Association (AERA) annual meeting in Denver and at the Critical Race Theory Conference in New York at Teachers College, Columbia University. Nicholas dedicates this book to his daughters Chloe Haejin (6), Avery Hana (4), and Olivia Eunhae (1). May it be possible that one day racism is dismantled for you girls.

FOREWORD

I grew up in a small town with little racial diversity. My brother and I were most often the only Black kids in varied crowds of White peers. Each year brought altercations rooted in racial bias and bigotry. The easy fights were the physical ones. Though this combat resulting from covert racism taxed the body, consequences were far less damaging than the effects *covert* racism had on my humanity, my soul, my mind. After these battles, my mother did her best to help me process my experiences, and, more importantly, to assist me in identifying the psychosis of my assailants. This process of identification, this ability to distinguish the enemy, has proven valuable as I traverse through myriad manifestations of systemic, individual, covert, and overt racism as an educator.

The ability to recognize and categorize oppression is rare given the current times. White supremacy is pervasive and often undetected. Its slick and mostly silent *modus operandi* affords an anonymity that often precludes people from naming the sources of their oppression. The assaults are most often swift and stinging, leaving the assaulted wounded and wondering, unable to accurately identify the assailant. This book offers a line-up of likely suspects.

A list of suspects is developed to explain the discriminatory treatment minoritized1 people in the United States often experience. Employing autoethnography, Whiteness is examined through the personal stories of eleven diverse authors. Their racial backgrounds, their lived experiences complicate perceptions of racism and trouble common tropes and frameworks typically used to understand race and racism. These explanative and counternarratives are important—especially now. Many want to believe that we live in a colorblind, post-racial society, yet oppression vigorously, creatively remains in most American institutions—especially schools. With race diminished as a viable mitigating factor influencing people's life trajectories, these authors contend that the marginalized are often left searching for explanations, looking for the source of the subjugation they suffer, and worse yet, internalizing felt hatred they experience. This work confronts those sources and explores the kind of conflict most avoided—self-conflict necessary for intrapersonal change.

This book is unique in that White supremacy is discussed, as a transferable equalizer. Cheryl Harris[2] positions Whiteness as property. Possession of this property, adoption of the norms and values of the dominant culture, affords benefits to those minoritized people who assimilate. The advantages, of course, do not equate to those with a White birthright; however, life is definitely different for those who cloak themselves in Whiteness and adopt the ways of white folk. The transformational power of Whiteness is alluring to minoritized people in search of a better life.

Even with my adverse encounters with White extremists and my mother's diligence in ensuring my knowledge of significant contributions made by people who look like me, schooling and societal messages that delineated and reinforced my racial inferiority led me to internalize racism, practice varying degrees of self-deprecation, and identify with Whiteness. Abandoning accountability to the collective, a value most aligned with the ethos people of color live by, I competed and won. The prize? I joined and contributed to oppressive systems. I found a success adopting Whiteness. Like the authors, I won by investing in the monocultural ethnocentrism I later interrogated and worked hard to unhook from.

Like me, these authors have their own stories, their own experiences with whiteness. They each offer perspectives of Whiteness and detail their varied journeys toward unhooking from Whiteness and its privileges, renouncing the advantages conformity to White supremacy has afforded them. Each author has made a commitment to antiracist work in unique ways, and their voices come from diverse cultural, racial, and professional historical spaces. This commitment to disconnect from privilege is wrought with complex contradictions as they continue this work while still enjoying and employing the accouterments of the Academy, one of the quintessential and iconic fortresses of White supremacy. Theirs are on-going journeys of evolving hypocrisies, tempered by reconciliations made with self in their battles against multiple forms of expedient systemic oppression. These stories have generalizable struggles from which we may all learn if we dare to endeavor in this work.

Read these stories with a self-critiquing lens. Consider the words of these writers with a frame of self-reflection. You're sure to find the stories compelling. As you turn the pages, read your own story within the lines offered. Do not neglect this opportunity to self-reflect. Engage yourself, your life's details. Search out your attachment, your dependence, your complicity with White supremacy and Whiteness, your participation with oppression. Examine your sources of privilege not just for the sake of knowing, but for the sake of leveraging that capital for the uplifting of those in need, those without your advantages, your influence, your voice.

Analyze Then MOVE

Do something. Move past what Dr. Martin Luther King, Jr. termed "the paralysis of analysis".[3] Read this book and know. We who know are then called to be people of conviction, not conformity. The knowledge of your role in promulgating White supremacy, your perpetuation of Whiteness from the ivory towers of the Academy, for example, should propel you to action. Social justice demands loyalty to the moral imperative of nonconformity. Schooling institutions, which portend to laud independent thought, are wrought with pressures to conform. Like me, like these authors, resist. Be not seduced by symbols of success fashioned by the dominant culture. Be willing to risk the comfort and security positioned in Whiteness. Determine your own metric by which you measure your accomplishments—your consistent work unhooking from Whiteness and abolishing White supremacy. Unhook and connect to humanity.

Rema Reynolds, Ph.D.
Educator, Activist, and Advocate
Spring 2013

NOTES

¹ *Minoritized*, unlike minority, emphasizes the process of *minoritizing* and insists that the relative prestige of cultures are constituted in social relations of power and agency (Mukherjee, et. al., 2006). Those who are *Minoritized*, unlike minority, emphasizes the process of *minoritizing* and insists that the relative prestige of cultures are constituted in social relations of power and agency (Mukherjee, et. al., 2006). Those who are minoritized are subordinated in power relations by those belonging to the dominant culture (Tettey & Puplampu, 2006).

² Harris, C. (1993). Whiteness as property. *Harvard Law Review, 106*, 1709–1791.

³ King, M. L., Jr. (2012). *A gift of love: Sermons from strength to love and other preachings.* Boston: Beacon Press.

CLEVELAND HAYES, BRENDA G. JUÁREZ,
MATTHEW T. WITT & NICHOLAS D. HARTLEP

1. TOWARD A LESSER SHADE OF WHITE

12 Steps Towards More Authentic Race Awareness

INTRODUCTION: HOW THIS ALL GOT STARTED

The impetus for this chapter was an email conversation between two academic colleagues at the University of Inland, both male, one Black (Malcolm[1]), the other White (Paul), and the response by a third faculty member from another college (George, who is also White).

It all started when Malcolm walked out of a teacher education diversity meeting in protest after a White faculty member made a flip comment about diversity (Juárez, Smith, & Hayes, 2008). Paul, being the instructor of the diversity class in the teacher credential program, subsequently engaged with Malcolm via email, setting the tone for what followed. Ultimately, after a series of email exchanges, Paul characterized Malcolm as a "Black Supremacist." Paul's comments, abbreviated, are as follows:

> I know that you are incredibly angry. Believe me: we all know that. It is always extremely evident how you feel. I personally perceive you to be an angry black supremacist, if there is such a thing. And I have to keep asking myself what I would do if you were a White supremacist instead, and my answer is the same: anger will not change anything. It never has. It never will.

Malcolm shared this email response with George, a White faculty member of another college. George emailed back to Malcolm with this tongue-in-cheek response:

> I didn't know you were a Black supremacist. Wow. It all makes sense now. What a relief. At first, I thought Paul was forcing equivalence between Black supremacist and White supremacist in a way only a White Ph.D. could pull off. Which would make Paul look really, really silly in a kind of spooky way, kind of like: [quoting Martin Luther King from Malcolm's email footer notes] "Nothing in the entire world is more dangerous than sincere ignorance and conscientious stupidity." Owww!! Oooops!! Whip me, beat me, make me conscientiously stupid!! Thanks, Paul, for leading the way with the first step backwards in the 12 Step Program for Whiteness. Remember: the first step backwards is the most important, and, unlike other 12 Step Programs, it's really not that hard to take. And remember White brethren: this is really critical for maintaining White privilege. So stand up to the Man and his Black

C. Hayes and N.D. Hartlep (Eds.), Unhooking from Whiteness:
The Key to Dismantling Racism in the United States, 1–16.
© 2013 Sense Publishers. All Rights Reserved.

nacy. Stand up, and walk backwards. Stand up White people! Stand up
walk the other way; because the farther you walk, the blacker the Black
.emacist gets. It's weird, but true. He looks blacker from a distance. And
u...t's what we all want, right? We all want to stop denying who we really are
and just walk backwards.

The University of Inland is a small private college in a suburb of Los Angeles. Paul,
who is White, teaches the diversity class in the teacher credential program. Malcolm,
who is Black, teaches the single subject methods course, but is an education
anthropologist and sociologist. Paul is what Hayes & Juárez (2009) classify as a
"good" White person trying to get a "good White people's medal" from Malcolm.

The idea for the title of the chapter came from the exchange between Paul and
Malcolm, an exchange that struck the authors as emblematic of what passes for
"authentic exchange" in the academy: a tokenized exchange that is demonstrably
one-sided and one-way.

HOW TO READ THIS CHAPTER

Following Thompson (2003), we put Whiteness at the center of our examination
of Malcolm's professional experiences as a teacher educator for social justice.
For the purposes of this paper, Whiteness is defined as an identity that is neither
problematized nor particularized within discourses on race because it assumes
a status of normalcy (Chaisson, 2004; DeCuir & Dixson, 2004; Tate, 2003).
Malcolm's questioning of Paul's desire for a "good White people medal" challenges
the legitimacy of Whiteness. Paul's actions toward Malcolm, by contrast, fail to
question Whiteness and thus reinforce it as legitimate and normal.

Malcolm's counter-narrative is a composite story made up of characters and events
based on actual individuals and situations to represent a particular kind of experience
common to and recognized by many scholars of color within higher education. In
this chapter, we explore how a critical reading of Malcolm's lived experiences can
become a learning tool for creating more authentic conversations around democratic
and inclusive forms of teaching and learning.

The diversity of the four researchers is identified because we draw from one of
the central tenets of Critical Race Theory (CRT), which is to cross epistemological
boundaries: CRT borrows from several intellectual traditions, including liberalism,
feminism, and Marxism, to construct a more complete analysis of "raced" people.
Apropos how CRT is interdisciplinary, the authors' experiences, expertise, and
disciplines come together in this essay (Dixson & Rousseau, 2006; Tate, 1997). Each
of us is committed to ending the racial oppression of those who claim not to be "one
of those White people" but then accuse someone of being a Black supremacist.

We used our experiential knowledge of Whiteness and racism to develop our
twelve-step program towards more authentic race awareness. The twelve steps,
in the context of this chapter, are a set of guiding principles outlining a course of
action as a way to address Whiteness. The intent of the chapter is not to attack

2

White people, as Whiteness is not about White people but is a mindset. Nor is the intent to imply that Whiteness is a psychological disorder. Rather, this paper intends to confront the socially constructed and constantly reinforced power of white identifications and interest (Bergerson, 2003; Gillborn, 2005). Our intent is to attack not individuals but an institution rooted with teacher education candidates and White faculty members who employ a wide range of speech genres and discourses to speak of self-declared marginalization that allows them to fend off the moral entanglements of White privilege and White racism (McCarthy, 2003). Using the 12-step metaphor, our critique of Whiteness is aimed at addressing equity issues and examining institutional practices (Green, Sonn, & Mastebula, 2007; Juárez, Smith, & Hayes, 2008; Tate, 2003).

COUNTER-STORIES AND CRITICAL STORYTELLING

How does Malcolm's counter-story connect people's daily lives with the privileging of Whiteness within U.S. society and its institutions? Counter-stories bridge the gap between societal structures of Whiteness and everyday life by revealing the ways institutional forces influence and guide individuals' daily interactions and practices.

Critical race counter-storytelling, in turn, is a method of recounting the experiences and perspectives of racially and socially marginalized people. Counter-stories reflect on the lived experiences of people of color as a way to raise critical consciousness about social and racial injustice. Counter-stories serve as an entry point for illustrating how poor and working class Black families fight interlocking race, class, gender, and spiritual oppression (Knight, Norton, Bentley & Dixon, 2005; Parker & Stovall, 2004; Yosso, 2006). Counter-stories, according to Delgado (1989), can be loosely described as the stories of out-groups, that is to say, groups whose marginality defines the boundaries of the mainstream—whose voice, perspective, and consciousness have been suppressed, devalued and abnormalized.

THE RESEARCHERS

Cleveland is a Black male from the southern part of the United States. He teaches in the teacher education program at the University of Inland. He received his Ph.D. in social foundations from the University of Utah. His research interests are Critical Race Theory, Whiteness Theory, and Social justice in teacher education. Although he works in a teacher education program, he does not classify himself as a teacher educator.

Brenda is a White female from the Midwest. She is also a member of the Church of Jesus Christ of Latter Day Saints. She too received her Ph.D. from the University of Utah and is a social justice educator. She began her higher education career in a Teacher Education program at Brigham Young University.

Matt is a White male from the Pacific Northwest. He completed his undergraduate training at one of the most liberal universities in the country. He completed his

3

Ph.D. at Portland State University. Matt has background in urban studies and public administration; his scholarship examines how Whiteness shapes public institutions outside of education.

Nicholas is a Korean Adoptee from the Midwest. He is a trained elementary education teacher. He completed his Ph.D. at the University of Wisconsin-Milwaukee. Nicholas has a background in Asian American studies, and his research interests include unhooking from Whiteness as coalition building and disrupting the model minority stereotype. He is a transracial adoption and model minority stereotype critic (Hartlep, 2013a, 2013b, 2013c, 2013d, 2013e, 2013f).

CONCEPTUAL FRAMEWORK: THE WHITE PROBLEM

What is it, then, about the democracy-racism paradox that connects democratic ideals to racialized exclusions? In 1968, after four years of inner city upheavals and riot, the U.S. National Advisory Commission on Civil Disorders (aka "the Kerner Commission"), which was authorized to report and give recommendations for addressing these matters to Congress and the President, delivered—without mincing rhetoric—this summary: "Segregation and poverty have created [within] the racial ghetto a destructive environment totally unknown to most White Americans. What White Americans have never fully understood – but what the Negro can never forget – is that White society is deeply implicated in the ghetto: White institutions created it, White institutions maintain it, and White society condones it" (Kerner, 1968, p. 2, as cited in Massey & Denton, 1997, p. 3). A three-pronged juggernaut of racist home mortgage lending policies, race-tiered public school financing, and Jim Crow-derived employment standards persisting through the 20th Century and beyond, are the White institutions to which the Kerner Report addressed its indictment. Nearly a half century earlier, the Chicago Commission on Race Relations had derived virtually identical conclusions following a riot there in 1919 after the drowning of a black youth by White assailants. Karl Marx once limned, "History repeats twice; first as tragedy, then as farce." The persistence of racialized exclusions within the context of much vaunted democratic ideals would seem to give testament to Marx's dictum.

Even by 1968, as Freund (2004) notes, "the structure of most federal housing and development agencies had barely changed, and the assumptions about the dual housing market, so long entrenched in practice and in bureaucratic culture, continued to guide federal operations" (p. 4). Moreover:

> For by the 1960s, state policy had not only helped to create a racially segregated, "dual" market for housing. It had also—quite paradoxically—helped convince whites that the government had done no such thing: that the growth of all-white suburbs and the concentration of black poverty in central cities were simply products of consumer choice in a free market for homes. …In short, federal policies had been instrumental to building both the segregated metropolis

and, with it, a political and economic constituency deeply resistant to change. To alter these government programs – as well as the "urban outcomes" that they had produced – would require more than executive orders [as President Kennedy had done in 1962] and a legislative ban against discrimination (Freund, 2004, pp. 4–5).

It would be against the self-sealing qualities these policies effected across a broad swath of the American White public that the Kerner report inveighed its criticism, challenging the conventional wisdom that inner-city ghettos were the exclusive product of free market activity *and not* the product of concerted, orchestrated, decades long practices of exclusionary land use zoning, race restrictive covenants, entrenched bureaucratic routines, captured and corrupted housing legislation, and the derivative and reciprocating effects of education and employment discrimination.

Karl Marx's dictum about tragedy turned farce derives more pointed, potent relevance for America through the lens of its black savants, as with *the White problem* (DuBois 1940/1968; Wright 1957), a concept derived from the black radical tradition (Dawson 1994; Olson 2004). Responding to a reporter's question about race relations in the U.S., Richard Wright (1946) famously explained, "There isn't any Negro problem; there is only a White problem" (cited in Kinnamon & Fabre, 1993, p. 99). By redefining U.S. society's race *problem* as White instead of black, "Wright called attention to its hidden assumptions—that racial polarization comes from the existence of blacks rather than the behavior of whites, that black people are a 'problem' for Whites rather than fellow citizens entitled to justice, and that, unless otherwise specified, 'American' means 'white'"(Lipsitz, 2006, p. 1).

Synchronous with how racist institution building obscured white culpability for the ghetto, Bennett (1972) comments, "It was a stroke of genius really for white Americans to give Negro Americans the name of their problem, thereby focusing attention on symptoms [the Negro and the Negro community] instead of causes [the White man and the White community]."(p. 1) Institutionalized and normalized as the right and natural way to interpret or understand the meaning of blackness, the hidden assumptions of *the White problem* created a particular social knowledge that racially marked being black (i.e., "Negro") as outside the tacit White norm and therefore a *problem* for whites. By racializing blackness through the privileging of characteristics and interests associated with Whites, *the White problem* both exculpated Whites from their collective and historical role in the systemic domination of African Americans and reassured whites that blacks had only themselves to blame for their impoverished situation. Stripped of context and history, in turn, *the White problem* incited, obscured, justified, and normalized incessant and pervasive violence against African Americans and other historically disenfranchised groups in the U.S. Pointedly, today's commonplace practices of police surveillance, housing segregation, job discrimination, and race-based ability grouping in schools reflect contemporary applications of *the White problem* enacted as U.S. society's contemporary People of Color *problem*.

5

If we want to understand what is happening in Harlem, to paraphrase Leronne Bennett, Jr. (1972), we must look to White America. By looking to White America, we see that it is the privileging of ideas, interests, values, beliefs, assumptions, images, and norms associated with Whites, that is to say, *the White problem*, which invents *the colorline* by joining social knowledge about "people of color as problem" with practices to become *knowledge practices* (Rose, 1989).

Defined as the "body of anonymous, historical rules, always determined in the time and space that have defined a given period" (Foucault, 1972, p.117), knowledge practices serve as interpretive lenses guiding the ways we talk about and conduct ourselves with regard to particular topics of interest (Barry, 1999; Hall, 1997). Knowledge of the classroom as an environment of "learning", for example, structures "how the teacher supervises classroom practices as well as a way in which teachers and children become self-governing in the spaces of schooling" (Popkewitz & Brennan, 1998, p. 9). Knowledge of African Americans as a *problem* likewise guides what educators and others deem reasonable and appropriate interactions and activities. In Alabama, for instance, African Americans make up 36% of the student population and 60% of the students expelled from the state's public schools (The Education Trust, 2006, p. 11). The concept of *driving while black* similarly illuminates punitive social practices disproportionately targeted at and experienced by African Americans (Feagin, 2001). Importantly, even the most technical social practices in schools and society carry a particular way of understanding the human beings who are the subjects and objects of talk and activity (Franklin, 1999; Hall, 1997; Rose, 1989).

THE 12 STEPS

Exactly what does it mean to unhook oneself from Whiteness? In this section, drawing from our experiential knowledge of Whiteness, we develop what we consider key steps to unhook from Whiteness. What is important for people to understand is that in 2013, people of color and their White allies are not typically being subjected to physical violence for attempting to upset Whiteness (as they were, say, in 1965). Nevertheless, as Malcolm X noted [as quoted in Gaskin (2006)], racism is like a Cadillac: a new model is produced every year. In other words, the persecution of those who upset Whiteness may no longer result in lynching, but it continues albeit in different [more insidiously subtle forms than those endured by so many during previous eras in their struggles for equality (Juárez & Hayes, In-Press).

The 12 Steps

Step one. Hello my name is [fill in the blank] and I have benefitted from racism. I have benefited from a racist world because I benefit from being White. I understand that Whiteness was invented and is maintained with a dominant and normal status to make "others" less privileged and powerful. I understand that all societies rank and tier social privileges. But in America, I understand that skin tone became the primary signifier for these privileges. This realization may be difficult for me but I must face my racist behavior and name the contours of racism (Bergerson, 2003; Dei, Karumanchery & Karumanchery-Luik; 2007; Gillborn, 2005).

This has been an historical process denoting the dominant subtext of the American experience. Because the "inalienable rights" claimed as pretext for revolution from British overlordship—freedom, equality, opportunity—have, in America, never been conferred symmetrically across class and race, so-called "inalienable rights" are de facto "wished for" rights, which have persevered as free floating signifiers for the "deserving Americans," those who "work hard and play by the rules." Among such rules is the one never spoken and therefore that much more assiduously obeyed: Never question the rules. This is an over-simplified parable on American democracy, but, as this essay will show, this parable is sufficient for giving account of how a race/class binary construction has determined who is privileged to speak about what, and for whom; as with how Paul presumes to tell Malcolm how and how not to behave, how and how not to succeed, how and how not to think about Malcolm's own experiences.

Step two. I do see color. I am not colorblind. Yes, King's dream metaphor, indeed, had a profound effect upon my psyche and I began to see race as invisible. However, the problem with this discourse is I am denying how the salience of race has continued to impede Americans of color from achieving socioeconomic parity with Whites. I have to understand that even though there have been profound legal changes in the social and economic status of blacks in general, racial discrimination persists in a number of social settings (Smith, 2008).

Step three. I cannot avoid what is uncomfortable. I cannot hide behind politeness and think I am working towards social justice. This will require much more than being nice to the brown people. It is more than teaching pre-service teachers to value and respect each individual kid by nurturing him/her in the way that he/she needs to be nurtured. Achieving social justice will require much more than simply placing emphasis on the "learning about students" assignments in my course or that I chose not to label something. If I don't put a label on "it," then it is not social justice. Also, as a White person I have the privilege to determine what gets labeled and what does not get labeled.

Step four. I am not afraid of angry Black or Latino male students. I should be angry myself and use their anger to make real change. I should be upset myself. We live in the wealthiest country in the world and yet Black students in Connecticut have test scores lower than kids in Moldova; students today are less likely to graduate from high school than their parents. I need to start making Whiteness uncomfortable by associating it with unexamined privileges and smug ignorance. If I do not disrupt the

7

coordinates determining how Whiteness effaces the rewards that should follow the virtue of an examined life, then I have not interrupted White supremacy.

Step five. I have to get over myself. It is not all about me. I should not expect love and a "good White people medal" (Hayes & Juárez, 2009) from those I oppress. It is not love when I express how much I love my Black friend; it is rather the inversion of human kinship based on mutual respect that can too often turn to racist contempt when the object of my fetishized self-concept rejects my fantasy. This contempt turns to anger manifested through elaborate channels that silence, exclude, and expel those who would not give me my fantasy; as, in the case of the academy, when tenure is denied. The number of Black and Latino males who actually achieve tenure on predominantly White college campuses is dismal at best.

Step six. I may "understand" White racism on one hand while on the other deny any entailment in its proliferation by connecting racism against minorities to my own "victim" status (i.e. "I'm a vegan and can't get a meal on campus," "I'm non-Mormon at a Mormon University," "I'm the only White in a Latin American country, while serving on my LDS mission"). I also proliferate racism by my silence when I do not challenge comments made by White pre-service teachers such as "Migrant farmer workers are not marginalized" and write them off as with "The student did not know" or "They need to learn." Worst of all is when I pretend to be liberal and to support equality, then allow White students to marginalize the Black professor because he requires them to engage in the "tough" conversations about race and equality (McCarthy, 2003).

Step seven. I have to understand when I am showing my Whiteness. I am showing my Whiteness when I argue we are moving too fast when a scholar from another university talks about White racism and on being Black at historically White institutions. I have to stop being regularly offended as demonstrated by an appallingly oppressive and bloody history known all over the world (Baldwin, 1985). Yet, after 244 years of slavery, 100 years of lynching, and 40 odd years of formal civil rights, I have to ask who is moving too fast? Lastly, I have to stop deciding how fast we should be going.

Step eight. I have to stop using the following statements: "Don't blow things out of proportion or get too pushy"; "Stop beating a dead horse and using race as a crutch"; "just let the race thing go and get over it"; "Stop being angry [with Whites]; "forgive [Whites] and forget about slavery." I have to understand that statements such as these fail to acknowledge the roles of power and difference in social formation. I have to understand that difference is constructed through racist discourses and hiding how power obscures culpability for oppression (Juárez, Smith & Hayes, 2008).

Step nine. I admit the possibility that my interests in helping marginalized people may be self-serving. I may not have a vested interest in the racial equality of marginalized groups unless that equality converges with my own self-interest, and I will tolerate the remedy of affirmative action only to the point that policy makers do not threaten my superior societal status (Bell, 2003).

Step ten. I have to convince females and non-White males to unite in support of Affirmative Action. As a White male, I am in fact the minority in the United States, where there are almost twice as many females and non-White males. What I need to realize is that if the United States axes affirmative action it will be my White mother, my White daughter, and my White significant other who will be left out. I understand that my support of Affirmative Action is not a moral obligation or a way for me to deal with my White guilt, but an appeal to protect the White women in my life. I understand that it is interest convergence that minorities will see some benefit but my intent is to give White women a chance (Tate, 2003).

Step eleven. I need to understand that this "clan" mentality continues to create a divide between Whites and people of color. "Clan" is the basic unit of all social organization. Following Maslow's theory of needs, "social belongingness" is a deficiency need, which means it is something we require in order to meet higher needs, and so take more or less for granted once it is met. Unlike higher order needs, social belongingness is not something we want to keep working at acquiring. For that matter, the signifiers for belonging are mostly non-verbal, pre-conscious. In the American context, skin tone is a potent signifier for who belongs "where" and "to whom." So out of this clan mentality, this binary construction around race—the surface, economic realities and the sub-surface psychosexual dimensions—have served a very potent and effective means for distracting White "consciousness" from ever confronting "the man."

Step twelve. I understand that Whiteness requires a constant distraction from the discovery of its hypocrisy. The more I claim to be a liberal, the more I show my Whiteness. Smith (2008) argues that the tenets of liberalism continue to influence new generations of young White Americans, particularly with respect to how individualism remains a major strand of thinking against a backdrop of colorblind racial ideology.

Social justice advocacy and achievement is not easy; it is often painful. Moreover, social justice is not some fad or new vocabulary term aimed at helping teacher education programs achieve national accreditation. Accrediting agencies must hold accountable educational institutions for examining social justice, and must be willing to deny program applicants accreditation that do not fulfill curriculum requirements addressing diversity and social justice. As an academy, we have to look at teacher education programs institutionally rather than individually. We [the authors] contend that social justice is more than "playing nice" as it relates to issues of diversity, social justice, and student access. Teacher education programs should have a fully detailed plan to address, for example, the dismal fact that Latino and Black males are not graduating from high school. Institutionally, we are failing this group of students.

DISCUSSION: SOME OTHER COMPARISONS
THAT ALWAYS NEED TO BE MONITORED

Using Reason and Evans' (2007) argument, Malcolm's frustrations stem from Paul's refusal to examine his own racial identities (or even to recognize that he is making such a refusal), as if racial discrimination is a thing of the past. Malcolm's justifiable frustrations will persist so long as the very nature of academic environments continues to perpetuate multiple characteristics that excuse White students and White faculty from seriously taking the time to examine the role of race in the lives of others, where Whiteness is a set of normative cultural practices.

This next list that we developed arises out of the notion that those individuals who are not engaged in overtly racist behavior are not racist (Bonilla-Silva, 2006). This list is grounded on the premise that Whites who refuse to challenge the true structural, institutional, and societal causes of inequity are as culpable of racist practices as are those who actively deny perpetuating these practices.

This list, which illustrates some common though often unconscious presumptions, is designed to present the realities of White*ness*. The fiction of "color-blindness" is deeply rooted in the belief that "good" White people can comfortably ignore race (Hayes & Juárez, 2009; Reason & Evans, 2007). This view is grounded in the ubiquitous, background, hegemony-vested "individuality" in the American cultural mythos. Our hope with this list is for us (people in academia) to move toward a more racially cognizant Whiteness, where White students and faculty members can have a space to identify themselves as White, to recognize the unearned advantages they accrue because of being White, and to demonstrate how their presumptive, unexamined privileges make them culpable for racist practices (Hytten & Warren, 2003; Reason & Evans, 2007; Urrieta, 2006).

1. White people have feelings. Black men are angry.
2. White people understand causes like the environment and world hunger. Black men are always too unhappy to notice these issues.
3. White people understand what it takes to work hard and they appreciate why defending our country and way of life requires us to fight in other countries. Black people act as if this country is not a safe place already, nor do they grasp that it is safe because of the hard work White politicians do helping us all fight elsewhere. (Notice how Barack Obama wants to "spread the wealth," as if that is not what we are doing when we bring democracy to other countries! Of course we have to shoot first! Someone has to take the first step towards Whiteness!)
4. Black people/men do not really all look the same. But this doesn't matter: they all think the same, which is really why they appear the same. White people are all different and unique individuals because we understand what's really important and why Black people are actually not really "Black"; they're just angry. This is a complex matter that can't really be explained unless it is already understood.
5. White people are not really White. Whiteness indicates correct attitudes emanating outwards.

6. White people suffer the anger of Black people because White people care. The more angry Black people get, the more White people care. Why Black people cannot see how much Whites care is just, well, the way things are. Which is why people-who-radiate-Whiteness, are who [we] are: because we care so much.
7. And so on. This is how this works. White people have to keep reciting to ourselves, "We are goodness." It will hurt doing so because Black people will just get angrier and angrier. But that's OK, because that's the way things are. Whiteness radiates goodness. Blackness brings that goodness out.

THESE ARE THE FACTS

According to McCarthy (2003), eighty-eight percent of the thirty-five thousand fulltime, regular, instructional faculty in the field of education are White; in the case of the University of Inland in the college of education, and more specifically in the teacher education program, out of a faculty of 60 there are four full-time faculty of color (three Blacks and one Latino). But as this relates to the premise of this chapter, McCarthy (2003) argues that White teachers and students benefit from a lack of faculty of color, because this White identity is an effect of privilege and material advantage. When faculty of color challenge this privilege, all too often they get identified as not being a well-behaved minority (Juárez, Smith, & Hayes, 2008) and their identities are constructed through negative discourses that are described as rude, hostile, angry. The perpetrators of these discourses around White racial micro-aggressions (Delgado & Stefancic, 2001) are never called to task.

Racism is a correlate of democracy (Cone, 2004; Delgado, 1999). When the immensity and depth of the physical and psychological violence continually committed against minoritized peoples are considered, the majority of it by *nice* people, we realize that the cost in suffering and lost lives is too high to keep tiptoeing around Whiteness and trying to appease and placate (otherwise decent) White people. We also realize that "[w]hat societies really, ideally, want is a citizenry which will simply obey the rules of society. If a society succeeds in this, that society is about to perish. The obligation of anyone who thinks of [herself or] himself as responsible is to examine society and try to change it and to fight it—at no matter what risk. This is the only hope society has. This is the only way societies change" (Baldwin, 1963, cited in Wise, 2005, p. 61). For democratic education to be realized, therefore, we must work together to abolish, rather than ignore, the Whiteness of teacher education.

The ongoing demographic shifts in the past three decades have led to the increased visibility of Asian Americans and Latinos (Pew Research Center, 2012). This increased visibility has brought new challenges to educators on how to go about understanding these communities' complex and diverse histories, cultural practices, and educational aspirations. As these two fastest-growing populations continue to emerge across the United States, educators must begin to interrogate the conventional wisdoms about race and race relations beyond the Black and White binary (Wing, 2007; Wu, 2002).

11

Scholars have argued that such binary is inadequate in explaining the educational experiences of these children and their families. As a consequence, the persistence of the Black-White paradigm has rendered the experiences of Asian Americans and Latinos invisible where their voices are often ignored and misunderstood (Pang & Cheng, 2000; Wing, 2007). Whiteness wants to maintain the Black-White binary since it is used as a tactic to divide-and-conquer, maintaining its power, and expanding its hegemony through "racial triangulation" (Kim, 1999).

In this book the authors through the use of autoethnographies (Reed-Danahy, 1997) highlight the importance of "unhooking from Whiteness" and of building coalitions as a strategy to disrupt Whiteness (Leonardo, 2009). Through their autoethnographies, the authors will identify some of the key issues facing antiracism work for African Americans, Whites, Asian Americans, and American Indians. The goal is to reconsider the strategies by which antiracist scholars do their work, as well as to provide pragmatic ways in which people—White and of color—can build cross-racial, cross-communal, and cross-institutional coalitions to fight White supremacy (Aoki, 2010).

Each chapter employing the qualitative methodology of auto-ethnography will illustrate the individual journey to unhook from Whiteness in order to fully participate in doing antiracist work. The chapters differ from the work of Peggy McIntosh (1988), since people of color also have to unhook from Whiteness. The chapters contend that in order to do authentic antiracist work, one must fully disengage from Whiteness. Leonardo (2009) argues antiracist work is not a commitment because one gains in human terms, but for Whites it actually means losing position in the racial hierarchy. The narratives chronicle the experiences of loss for whites and the movement towards a critical analysis of our own oppression for people of color. The journey to unhook from Whiteness is different, the loss is different, but the outcomes are the same: racial justice.

Brenda Juárez's chapter entitled *Learning to Take the Bullet and More: Anti-racism Requirements for White Allies and Other Friends of the Race, So-Called and Otherwise* considers the historical tensions of White anti-racism in struggles for racial justice. Drawing on her own struggles and the collective wisdoms of the Black radical traditions in the US, the author interrogates her own journey in attempting to move away from and unhook herself from Whiteness by analyzing the limits, possibilities, and consequences of the choices she has made over time in her personal and professional life as she has worked to help push forward endeavors of racial justice. The author posits that the anti-racism efforts of Whites will continue to reinforce the historical privileging of the interests of White people as a racial group unless sincere White people of goodwill keep working to disrupt the structures of White privileges until other Whites representing and acting in behalf of the existing racial hierarchy either expel them from the context or begin making more inclusive, justice-based changes (West, 1997).

Karla Martin's chapter entitled *Privileging Privilege with the Hope of Accessing Privilege* is an autoethnographic narrative written in letter format. As an assistant professor of educational foundations, Martin, a Native American activist, writes about how she is beginning to understand the ways that academia is entrenched in the privilege and power that upholds a system of Whiteness that automatically benefits some and fails others. She actively unhooks from Whiteness by remembering that her community is where her allegiances lie, and it is with them that she finds love, peace, comfort, and family. In short, she refuses to be a pawn for Whiteness as the only Native American in her department.

Nicholas Hartlep's chapter entitled, *I Refuse to Be a Pawn for Whiteness: A Korean Transracial Adoptee Speaks Out* is an autoethnographic narrative intended to dispel the model minority. The personal journey of a Korean American transracial adoptee is shared. The author discusses how his dual consciousness impacts his personal and professional approach to antiracist work. His narrative shares how he refuses to be used by Whiteness. In other words, the author refuses to acquiesce and benefit from honorary White status. Instead, he actively fights racism through forming coalitions with other people of color in hopes to undermine the model minority stereotype's divide-and-conquer strategy for maintaining white supremacy.

Kenneth Fasching-Varner, Margaret-Mary Dowell, Dana Bickmore and Steven Bickmore, in their chapter entitled *Repositioning the hook: (Re)committing to equity through autoethnographic exploration,* examine how they unhook from Whiteness as White allies. Through an autoethnographic lens, four vignettes shared in this chapter examine intersecting ways in which Whiteness operates. Specifically, the vignettes show that despite commitment and expertise in anti-racism, racism emerges indicating ways in which each of the authors was socialized. The authors counter argue that one can never really unhook from Whiteness, but rather can identify how they are implicated in Whiteness as a means to counteract White privilege and hegemony. The paper recommits faculty to equity and excellence in education as a means of addressing the individual and institutional problems of race.

Matthew Witt writes the chapter, *English Ivy*. This autoethnography examines encounters with race in the author's early life and adult graduate school and professional experience. From early experiences growing up in Portland, Oregon, cradled by 5,000 acres of urban forest park, to dawning awareness about what race signified across the river, Witt weaves in commentary on his parentage and family exodus—father from Dust Bowl Texas Panhandle, mother from post war Germany. Gleaning insights where he can from across an inter-generational tableau, the author threads this stream of consciousness utilizing the metaphor of English Ivy, known for its tenacious grip on soil and invasive properties across vulnerable plant terrain. The manner in which White consciousness has evolved, and the expansive tendencies that White privilege endows, is canvassed in the closing section.

Cleveland Hayes, author of the chapter *Too White to be Black and too Black to be White,* shares his "unhooking" and the academic lynching that ensued. During this presentation using auto-ethnographic methods, he presents his journey from Whiteness—the good, the bad, and the ugly—and how this has impacted his work as a social justice/anti racist educator. In his journey, he compares and contrasts his respective pasts and journeys of learning to struggle against the systemic privileging of Whiteness while living his life and enacting his work within historically White institutions. His purpose is to draw on his personal and professional experiences to identify and critically analyze the key factors and events that have influenced not only who he is today as an individual and teacher educator, but also the kinds of opportunities and limitations he has had to date. Analyzing the points at which different lived experiences converge, he ultimately illuminates the *modus operandi* of Whiteness as racial knowledge through and within moments when individuals and groups invoke their institutional authority to act, interact, and make decisions that help either to further or to challenge White supremacy. He submits that although his journey from Whiteness has led him down different paths, his journey from Whiteness has been a struggle.

Rosa Mazurett-Boyle and René Antrop-González, in their chapter entitled, *Our Journeys as Latin@ Educators and the Perpetual Struggle to Unhook from Whiteness* narrate personal and professional experiences of two U.S. Latin@s. They start with their trajectory into the field of education and, most importantly, why they continue teaching both at the high school and college levels. They reflect on their encounters with Whiteness, its influence on their Latin@ worldviews, and their pains to unhook from Whiteness in order to take ownership of their hybridity. Their worldviews place a high premium on Latin@ Community Cultural Wealth (Yosso, 2006). Consequently, they analyzed auto-ethnographic and interview data through the lens of Resistance Capital. The implications of their work are to support efforts to challenge dominant norms in the field of education and to set a course toward deeper and broader changes in the way K-16 educational systems conceptualize and validate the social and cultural wealth of non-dominant students, teachers, educators, and researchers.

By using autoethnographic methodologies, our attempt with the chapters in this book is to interrupt the racial triangle by describing our process of unhooking from Whiteness as a way to build coalition in hopes of ending racism in the United States. Whiteness continues to prosper when it keeps marginalized groups at odds with each other. This discourse can be seen in a historical context after the Civil War. DuBois (1935) argues that when the Civil War ended, White land owners created a social order that prevented poor Whites from joining political forces with the freed slaves. The contributors in this book representing the major minority groups and White allies hope that their stories will disrupt that social divide between these groups for the greater good. We will thus no longer become pawns to benefit Whiteness and to grease the capitalist machine. Lastly, for our efforts to end White supremacy to be truly effective, change must be fundamentally linked to collective effort to transform those structures that reinforce and perpetuate white supremacy (hooks, 1994).

NOTE

[1] All of the names in the narratives are pseudonyms. The University of Inland is also fictitious.

REFERENCES

Aoki, A. L. (2010). Coalition Politics. In E. W. Chen & G. J. Yoo (Eds.) *Encyclopedia of Asian American issues today* (volume 2) (pp. 707–712). Santa Barabara, CA: Greenwood Press.

Bell, Lee A. (2003). Telling tales: What stories can teach us about racism. *Race Ethnicity and Education, 6*(1), 3–28.

Bennett, L. (1972). The White problem in America. In Bennett, L. A. Jr. (Ed.) *The challenge of Blackness.* Chicago: Johnson Publishing Company, Inc.

Bergerson, A. A. (2003). Critical race theory and white racism: Is there room for White scholars in fighting racism in education? *Qualitative Studies in Education, 16*(1), 51–63.

Bonilla-Silva, E. (2006). *Racism without racists: Colorblind racism and the persistence of racial inequality in America.* Lanham, MD: Rowman and Littlefield.

Carter, S., Honeyford, M., McKaskle, D., Guthrie, F., Mahoney, S., & Carter, G. (Spring 2007). What do you mean by Whiteness?: A professor, four doctoral students, and a student affairs administrator explore Whiteness. *College Student Affairs Journal, 26*(2), 152–159.

Cone, J. H. (2004). Martin and Malcolm and America: A dream or a nightmare. Maryknoll, NY: Orbis Books.

Dawson, Michael C. (1994). A Black counterpublic?: Economic earthquakes, racial Agenda(s), and Black politics, *Public Culture, 7*, 195–223.

Dei, G. J. S., Karumanchery, L. L., & Karumanchery-Luik, N. (2007). *Playing the race card: Exposing White power and privilege.* New York: Peter Lang.

Dixson, A. D., & Rousseau, C. K. (2006). *Critical race theory in education.* New York: Routledge.

DuBois, W. E. B. (1940/1968). Dusk of dawn: An essay toward an autobiography of a race concept. New York: Schocken Books.

Feagin, J. R. (2001). *Racist America.* New York: Routledge.

Foucault, M. (1972). *The archaeology of knowledge and the discourse on language.* (A. M. Sheridan Smith, Trans.). New York: Pantheon.

Franklin, Barry. (1999). Discourse, rationality, and educational research: A historical perspective of RER. *Review of Educational Research 69*(4), 347–363.

Freund, D. M. P. (2004). Democracy's unfinished business: Federal policy and the search for fair housing, 1961–1968. Report submitted to the Poverty and Race Research Action Council, June 22, 2004. Retrieved September 15, 2005, from http://www.prrac.org/pdf/freund.pdf.

Gillborn, D. (2005). Education policy as an act of White supremacy: Whiteness, critical race theory and education reform. *Journal of Education Policy, 20*(4), 485–505.

Green, M. J., Sonn, C. C., & Matsebula, J. (2007). Reviewing Whiteness: Theory, research and possibilities. *South African Journal of Psychology, 37*(3), 389–419.

Hall, Stuart. (1997). *Representation: cultural representations and signifying practices.* Thousand Oak Critical race theory in education s, CA: Sage.

Hayes, C., & Juárez, B. G. (2009). You showed your Whiteness: You don't get a good White people medal. *International Journal of Qualitative Studies in Education, 22*(6), 729–744.

Hartlep, N. D. (2013a). *The model minority stereotype: Demystifying Asian American success.* Charlotte, NC: Information Age Publishing.

Hartlep, N. D. (2013b). *Policy suggestions for combating the Asian American model minority stereotype. Diverse: Issues in higher education.* Retrieved from http://diverseeducation.com/article/53192/

Hartlep, N. D. (2013c). *The model minority stereotype reader: Critical and challenging readings for the 21st century.* San Diego, CA: Cognella Publishers.

Hartlep, N. D. (2013d). The model minority? Stereotypes of Asian-American students may hurt more than they help. *Diverse: Issues in Higher Education, 30*(2), 14–15.

Hartlep, N. D. (2013e). The model minority stereotype: What 50 years of research does and does not tell us. *Diverse: Issues in Higher Education.* Retrieved from http://diverseeducation.com/article/52979/

Hartlep, N. D. (2013f). Why the model minority stereotype is divisive to all communities of color. *Diverse: Issues in Higher Education.* Retrieved from http://diverseeducation.com/article/52866/#

hooks, b. (1994). *Killing rage.* New York: Henry Holt.

Hyland, N. (2005). Being a good teacher of Black students? White teachers and unintentional racism. *Curriculum Inquiry, 35*(4), 429–459.

Hytten, K., & Warren, J. (2003). Engaging Whiteness: How racial power gets reified in education. *International Journal of Qualitative Studies in Education, 16*(1), 65–89.

Juárez, B. G., & Hayes, C. (2010). Social justice is not spoken here: Examining the nexus of knowledge and democratic education. *Power and Education, 2*(3), 233–252.

Juárez, B. G., Smith, D. T., & Hayes, C. (2008). Social justice means just us White people: The diversity paradox in teacher education. *Democracy & Education, 17*(3), 20–25.

Juárez, B. G., Smith, D. T., & Ball, N. M. (2009). *White rules for well-behaved minorities: Reasoning about the contemporary U.S. democracy-racism connection in education.* Unpublished manuscript

Juárez, B. G., Smith, D. T., & Hayes, C. (2008). *An open letter to White educators: On how Whiteness sabotages social justice in teacher preparation programs.* Unpublished manuscript.

Kerner, O. (1968). *The Kerner report.* New York: Pantheon Books.

Kim, C. J. (1999). The Racial Triangulation of Asian Americans. *Politics & Society, 27*(1), 105–138.

Kinnamon, K., & Michel, F. (1993). *Conversations with Richard Wright.* Jackson: University Press of Mississippi.

Leonardo, Z. (2009). *Race, Whiteness, and education.* New York, NY: Routledge.

Lipsitz, G. (2006). The possessive investment in Whiteness: How White people profit from identity politics. Philadelphia: Temple University Press.

Massey, D. S., & Denton, N. A. (1997). *American apartheid: Segregation and the making of the underclass.* Cambridge, MA: Harvard University Press.

McCarthy, C. (2003). Contradictions of power and identity: Whiteness studies and the call of teacher education. *International Journal of Qualitative Studies in Education, 16*(1), 127–133.

McIntosh, P. (1988). *Unpacking the invisible knapsack.* Retrieved on July 4, 2012 from http://www.nymbp.org/reference/WhitePrivilege.pdf

Olson, J. (2004). *The abolition of white democracy.* Minneapolis: University of Minnesota Press.

Pang, V. O., & Cheng, L.-R. L. (1998). *Struggling to be heard: The unmet needs of Asian Pacific American children.* Albany, NY: State University of New York Press.

Pew Research Center. (2012). *The rise of Asian Americans.* Washington, DC: Pew Social & Demographic Trends. Retrieved on June 24, 2012 from http://www.pewsocialtrends.org /files/2012/06/SDT-The-Rise-of-Asian-Americans-Full-Report.pdf

Popkewitz, T., & Brennan, M. (1998). *Foucault's challenge: Discourse, knowledge, and power in education.* New York: Teachers College Press.

Reason, R., & Evans, N. (2007). The complicated realities of Whiteness: From color blind to racially cognizant. *New Directions for Student Services.*

Reed-Danahy, D. E. (1997). *Auto/ethnography: Rewriting the self and the social.* New York, NY: Oxford University Press.

Rose, N. (1989). *Governing the soul.* New York: Free Association Books

Smith, D. T. (2009). *Compare and contrast how white racial attitudes and white racial ideology have been used in the research literature to understand contemporary forms of color-blind racism.* Unpublished Manuscript.

Tate, W. F. (1997). Critical race theory and education: History, theory, and implications. *Review of Research in Education, 22*, 195–247.

Tate, W. F. (2003). The "race" to theorize education: who is my neighbor? *International Journal of Qualitative Studies in Education, 16*(1), 121–126.

The Education Trust, Inc. (Fall, 2006). *Education watch Alabama.* www.edtrust.org. Downloaded 10/23/08.

Urrieta, L. (2006). Community identity discourse and the heritage academy: Colorblind educational policy and White supremacy. *International Journal of Qualitative Studies in Education, 19*(4), 455–476.

Wing, J. Y. (2007). Beyond black and white: The model minority myth and the invisibility of Asian American students. *The Urban Review, 39*(4), 455–487.

Wise, T. (2005). *White like me: Reflections on race from a privileged son.* Brooklyn, NY: Soft Skull Press.

Wright, R. (1957). *White man, listen!* New York: Anchor Books.

Wu, F. H. (2002). *Yellow: Race in America beyond black and white.* New York, NY: Basic Books.

CLEVELAND HAYES

2. TOO WHITE TO BE BLACK AND TOO BLACK TO BE WHITE

A Journey away from Whiteness

I NEVER SAW IT AS NEEDING TO UNHOOK

In 2010, Bonilla-Silva asked the question: Are Blacks colorblind, too? Colorblindness for Black people, in my opinion, serves the purposes of Whiteness. Blacks—me individually at one point—who subscribe to these discourses can be dangerous to anti-racist work because colorblind discourses are the ones Whites listen to as the model of behavior for all minority groups: Black Republicans come to mind as an example of how they become the spokespeople for all Black people.

Bonilla-Silva (2010) contends that Black people are affected by colorblind discourses differently, and the consequence for this discourse is developing an all out oppositional ideology to color-blind racism. The answer to this question is not rhetorical in nature as it pertains to my own personal experience. However, before getting started with describing my journey from Whiteness, this chapter is not intended to essentialze this one experience into the experiences of all Blacks and, more specifically, all Black men. In this chapter, I am only talking about one experience—mine—and my own continuing journey from Whiteness.

So, yes, Blacks are colorblind! I started school just as the schools in Mississippi were desegregating. I had White teachers and White friends who, at the time, I thought saw me for me. I worked hard; I was not disrespectful; I took ownership for my academic shortcomings; and, most importantly, I never played the race card. I did not want to be seen as a one of "those" Blacks. I was hooked on this notion that I would obtain the benefits of being White if I did what Whites did. It took me 35 years to realize that it is never going to happen.

In this chapter, using auto-ethnographic methods, I present my journey—the good, the bad, and the ugly—from Whiteness and how this has impacted my work as a social justice/anti racist educator. I compare and contrast my respective pasts and journeys of learning to struggle against the systemic privileging of Whiteness while living my life and enacting my work within historically White institutions. My purpose is to draw on my personal and professional experiences to identify and critically analyze the key factors and events that have influenced not only who I am today as an individual and teacher educator, but also the kinds of opportunities and limitations I have had to date. Analyzing the points at which

C. Hayes and N.D. Hartlep (Eds.), Unhooking from Whiteness:
The Key to Dismantling Racism in the United States, 17–31.
© *2013 Sense Publishers. All Rights Reserved.*

different lived experiences converge, I ultimately illuminate the *modus operandi* of Whiteness as racial knowledge through and within moments when individuals and groups invoke their institutional authority to act, interact, and make decisions that help to further or to challenge White supremacy. I submit that although my journey has led me down different paths, my journey from Whiteness has been a struggle.

In this chapter, I begin with how Critical Race Theory (CRT) became my beacon of light down the dark road of unhooking from Whiteness. Then, framed in the resistance work of Delgado Bernal and Solórzano (2001), I describe how I was trying to protect myself from the assault of Whiteness and the loss that came with trying to protect myself. In the section that follows, I will describe an instance when I began unhooking from Whiteness and the academic lynching that followed. I end my chapter by describing how CRT continues to guide my work as an anti-racist educator as well as my continuing struggles with unhooking.

UNDERSTANDING WHITENESS: A CRITICAL RACE PERSPECTIVE

For this chapter, I will use the tenets of Critical Race Theory (CRT) as the tool for dissecting my journey from Whiteness. Understanding CRT, like Knaus (2009), gave me the voice and narrative to challenge racism and the structures of oppression while advocating for social justice in its many forms, especially in my classroom (Hartlep, 2010). Tate (1997) asks the question, "Pivotal in understanding CRT as a methodology, what role should experiential knowledge of race, class and gender play in educational discourse?" (p. 235). Especially in the case of this chapter, I expand that question: How has unhooking from Whiteness changed my approach to teaching and advocating for those students who have no voice? Ladson-Billings (1998) states that CRT focuses on the role of "voice in bringing additional power and experiential knowledge that people of color speak regarding the fact that our society is deeply structured by racism" (p. 13). How has unhooking from Whiteness allowed me to give voice to students who do not have a voice, and how has unhooking from Whiteness allowed me to hear other voices such as those who, in one form or another, have already unhooked or refused to hook in the first place? In the case of K-12 education, this unhooking or refusal to hook comes in many forms: Often these kids are labeled as the disinterested other, and because I was hooked I contributed to this labeling.

In a similar vein, Solórzano and Yosso (2001) define CRT as "an attempt to understand the oppressive aspects of society in order to generate societal and individual transformation and [it is] important for educators to understand that CRT is different from any other theoretical framework because it centers race" (pp. 471–472). As a result, CRT scholars have developed the following tenets to guide CRT research, and all of these tenets are utilized within the design and analysis of this study (Kohli, 2009):

Centrality of Race and Racism

All CRT research within education must centralize race and racism, as well as acknowledge the intersection of race with other forms of subordination (Kohli, 2009; Sleeter & Delgado Bernal, 2002). As my narrative will show, CRT is my way to interpret and de-center Whiteness in the larger society. In order to forge partnerships in the fight for social justice, I also had to begin a critique of our own Whiteness. I did this by first de-centering Whiteness from my own life.

Valuing Experiential Knowledge

Solórzano and Yosso (2001) argue that CRT in educational research recognizes that the experiential knowledge of students of color is legitimate, appropriate, and critical to understanding, analyzing, and teaching about racial subordination in the field of education. Life stories tend to be accurate according to the perceived realities of subjects' lives. They are used to elicit structured stories and detailed lives of the individuals involved (Delgado, 1989; McCray, Sindelar, Kilgore, & Neal, 2002).

Fairbanks (1996) states that storytelling, one of the methodologies of CRT, has been an accepted mode of constructing realities throughout human history. CRT narratives and storytelling provide readers with a challenging account of preconceived notions of race. The thick descriptions that emerge from the stories serve to illuminate the experiences of the person telling the story (Parker & Lynn, 2002). Stories offer descriptions and explanations of situations and circumstances from which readers may cull insights into their own practices. For example, storytelling is about human agents doing things on the basis of beliefs and desires, striving for goals, and meeting obstacles (Fairbanks, 1996).

Challenging the Dominant Perspective

CRT research works to challenge dominant narratives, often referred to as majoritarian stories. CRT scholar Harris (1995) describes the "valorization of Whiteness as treasured property in a society structured on racial caste" (p. 277). Harris (1995) also argues that Whiteness conferred tangible and economically valuable benefits, and it was jealously guarded as a valued possession. This thematic strand of Whiteness as property in the United States is not confined to the nation's early history (Frankenberg, 1993; Ladson-Billings, 1998).

Unhooking from Whiteness" for me means centering the problem of White racism and refusing to place the onus on communities of color to fix the problem that they did not create. Whiteness, which I describe in my narrative, caused me to take ownership of "fixing" my communities, in hopes of obtaining some sort of validation. "Unhooking from Whiteness," for people of color, forces Whites to move away from a discourse of White racism to a discourse of Whiteness because

White racism is inherently oppressive but Whiteness is multifaceted and complex (Hayes & Juárez, 2009; Kendall, 2006; Leonardo, 2009).

This is an important distinction to understand. Many believe in general anti-discriminatory principles, that "color makes no difference," "people are people," and "there should be one human race" (Caditz, 1977). Many of the teachers in this group, according to Caditz (1977), have a strong and longstanding commitment to ethnic integration. They believe in the general ideas of civil rights and justice for minorities. In her study she described how even though many Whites felt themselves liberal, a majority of them voting for Johnson and Kennedy, their thinking did not match their practice. Many of the White participants in her study felt that having Black students attend schools within their White neighborhoods would lessen the value of their schools. These same White liberals felt unsafe around Black students, especially Black male students. Even though many White Americans felt the era of Jim Crow was wrong and worked to end this reign of tyranny in the South, as Caditz (1977) showed, they still devalued Blackness, illustrating the value that was still associated with being White. Black children are literally inundated with images that associate authority, beauty, goodness, and power with Whiteness (Hill, 2001).

Commitment to Social Justice

Social justice must always be a motivation behind CRT research. Part of this social justice commitment must include a critique of liberalism, claims of neutrality, objectivity, color-blindness, and meritocracy as a camouflage for the self-interest of powerful entities of society (Tate, 1997). Only aggressive, color-conscious efforts to change the way things are done will do much to ameliorate misery (Delgado & Stefancic, 2001; Tate, 1997).

Being Interdisciplinary

According to Tate (1997), CRT crosses epistemological boundaries. It borrows from several traditions, including liberalism, feminism, and Marxism to include a more complete analysis of "raced" people. Ladson-Billings (1998) has already put forth the argument that CRT has a place within education. She argues that CRT in education allows for the use of parables, chronicles, stories, and counterstories to illustrate the false necessity and irony of much of current Civil Rights doctrine: we really have not gone as far as we think we have. Adopting CRT as a framework for educational equity means that we will have to expose racism in education and propose radical solutions for addressing the ever-present issue (Ladson-Billing, 1998).

SAVING MYSELF FROM WHITENESS: RESISTING, OR WAS I?

I graduated from high school and went to Mississippi State. It was during college when my identity shifted. I took on the identity that Fordham (1996) describes in her book *Blacked Out*. At the time I really did not realize it; I thought what I was doing is what successful Black students did. I never realized how racist it was for someone to tell me, "You aren't really Black," or "If only more Blacks could be like you." This is the period of my life that I call too White to be Black and too Black to be White. In my mind I was thinking *if I am going to make it in the world, I have to ignore a certain part of my "Blackness."* I still attended a Black church and I had Black friends, but whenever the Black students organized themselves in order to fight a racial injustice I was not going to be there. I was acting White.

Delgado Bernal and Solórzano (2001) argue for four types of resistance. Their study provides a distinction between four different types of students' oppositional behavior: (1) reactionary behavior, (2) self-defeating resistance, (3) conformist resistance, and (4) transformational resistance (p. 13). However, for the purposes of this chapter and my journey from Whiteness, I will only focus on conformist resistance and transformational resistance; the other two were never part of my identity and journey from Whiteness because I knew early own that self-defeating resistance was not going to get me the what I perceive to be the benefits of Whiteness.

I Will Accept Your Domination Now: Conformist Resistance

Among contemporary African-Americans, resistance is constructed as power and appears to take two primary forms: conformity and avoidance. As conformity, it is interpreted as unqualified acceptance of the ideological claims of the larger society; within the African-American community, it is often perceived as disguised warfare in which the Black Self "passes" as (an) other in order to reclaim an appropriated humanity (Fordham, 1996, p. 39)

This type of resistance refers to the oppositional behavior of students who are motivated by social justice, yet hold no critique of the systems of oppression. These students want social change for themselves as well as for others, but are likely to blame themselves, their families, or their culture for the negative personal and social conditions. Though some social change is possible through conformist resistance, without a critique of the social, cultural, and economic forms of oppression, it does not offer the greatest possibility for social justice (Delgado Bernal & Solórzano, 2001).

Growing up, it never dawned on me that racism was endemic in American society. I had White friends. I had White teachers. It was not until I started school that things changed for me. I started to notice that some of the White kids received attention that I was not receiving but I wanted. It never dawned on me that the segregating factor was academics. My teachers had always told me that I was doing okay. I was passing. This is when my mother and I had a serious heart-to-heart about objectivity and neutrality. She told me, "You cannot just get C's; I know you can do better; you are going to do better; you are a young Black male; you are held to a different standard."

I thought she was the devil. I responded, "Racism is over, why don't you give it a rest?" However, some years later what she said had come to pass. I was in the ninth grade preregistering for 10th grade. In 10th grade students had to make a decision about what track they were going to take. I knew I was going to college; it had been an expectation in my family for years, and I was not going to be the exception. The school counselor had other ideas. She felt, based on my grades, that I should go the vocational route, and if it was not for my mother and father I would be working a factory job. From that day forward, thoughts around my identity changed. This experiential knowledge caused me to cross epistemological boundaries. I had to become more aware of what was going on around me. The subtle racism that was about to marginalize me, and the systems continuing the protection of Whiteness even though we were all supposed to be equal, are two examples.

I Won't Do It to Myself

My portrait looks at issues around identity, resistance, and what it meant to grow up as a Black man in Mississippi. My narrative takes me on a journey as a young man who felt that becoming as White-like as possible was the key to my success; it was me who needed to change, and it was my students, when I started teaching. Working to change the system was not a part of my thinking.

When the slaves received their First Emancipation, Black people constructed acting White as a characteristic of those group members who resisted affiliation with Blackness, with the slave experience, and with other Black people in exchange for success. This strategy compelled an uncritical resistance—manifested as conformity—to the then dominant ideology (Fordham, 1996). Likewise, I conformed as a way to achieve. I also conformed as a way to erase some of the negative stereotypes that dominant society has about Blacks. Again, I was looking at success through a Eurocentric lens (pull yourself up—isolate yourself from those unlike you—be more like us). I also conformed in hopes of cashing in on what I have now learned is "Whiteness as property." I conformed as a way to get "in," a way to get the management job, so I thought I would be able make the necessary social changes from the inside. Little did I know that Whiteness would not allow me because once I got the "card" to the club I was going to have to behave in certain ways in order to keep the "card." However, Fordham (1996) argues, when students take on this identity, when Black students strive to become an Other, they usually discover that their efforts are thwarted and their ability to both imagine and dominate is hyphenated and fragmented. A student in her study describes his experience that was not unlike my own personal experiences.

In college, I never understood why my White friends who claimed neutrality and meritocracy often left me out. There were several examples such as the case when I was passed over for a promotion to assistant residence hall director even though I was the most qualified and had the most experience among those applying. I played the game, working hard, and it didn't get me anywhere. At the time of these experiences, it didn't dawn on me that this was as a systematic position and nothing that I had done or did not do.

The student in Fordham's study states,

> I stayed in school and remained home at nights....I suffered a lonely Catholic school education.... At Notre Dame and Brown, I endured further isolation.... I burned the midnight oil as Dr. King had suggested.... I have a White education, a White accent, I conform to White middle-class standards in virtually every choice.... I led a square life ... and now I see that I am often treated the same as a thug, that no amount of conformity, willing or unwilling, will make me the fabled American individual (Fordham, 1996, pp. 51–52).

Black students resist dominant claims of Black intellectual inadequacy by conforming to existing norms and values. They work hard to disprove Black *lack*. These students struggle with images of "acting White" and with conceptions of book-Black Blacks. Book-Black Blacks are individuals whose identity is de-contextualized and constructed largely from academic and proper texts rather than from intimate interactions with African-Americans. Conforming to school norms propels them to a place where they are construed by their classmates as representing the dominant other (Fordham, 1996).

As the young man stated above, "no matter how much conforming I did, I was and I am still Black." When White people see me the first thing they see is Black, and then I will have to expend needless energies trying to disprove how Black I am. Conforming, in my opinion, only divides and allows dominant society to conquer. Those students who try to conform to dominant ideologies are socially removed, either by choice or by their peer groups. Therefore, conforming is not the sole answer. It may work in the short term, but long term effects (being removed from the fictive kinship) far outweigh any short term gains (Fordham, 1996).

I Won't Let the System Do It to My Students

Delgado, Bernal, and Solórzano (2001) argue external transformational resistance involves a more conspicuous and overt type of behavior, which does not conform to institutional or cultural norms. This type of resistance refers to a person's behavior that illustrates both a critique of oppression and a desire for social justice. In other words, for me as I started moving from Whiteness, I became aware of not only my oppressive conditions but also aware of the way the system was creating a permanent underclass. My motivations became less about White approval and more about social justice.

It was not until I began the journey of completing a Ph.D. that my approach toward students changed, and my own personal journey from Whiteness commenced. My approach has not changed in the sense that I am also "old school." I am a very demanding teacher with very high expectations, and I will not compromise my position. Because I teach in Salt Lake City, the number of Black students I teach is small in comparison to that in the South. I do share being a person of color with a large number of my students of color. Crossing epistemological boundaries,

I now have to take into account language and issues of immigration and class when I develop my teaching approach.

The internalization of Whiteness framed my philosophy when I first started to teach. I first started teaching in Mississippi right after I graduated from Mississippi State. Because of this Whiteness internalization, I felt that in order for students of color to be successful they were going to have to learn how to play the game, which meant in my mind basically not acting Black. I was looking at the students in a deficit mode; in other words, the reason why the students of color in my classes were not successful was their fault. When I moved to Utah and started teaching in Salt Lake City, I still went into my classroom with the deficit mindset toward students. I still believe that students have to be the best that they can be, and that the reason why they may or may not be is not necessarily something they are doing or not doing. I still believe that too many students of color are becoming victims of a school system that really does not believe that students of color, especially those who live on the wrong side of the street, can learn at a level comparable to that of White students.

Transformational resistance was and is the best type of resistance for me; as I began to unhook from Whiteness, it allowed me the freedom to socially change. Now, this does not come at a cost, which I will explain in the next section, but Leonardo (2010) argues that in order to move from Whiteness or to end Whiteness one has to be willing to lose, as many of the contributors in this project have expressed (c.f. Hartlep's chapter). In my opinion, that is what education is for, to make a change in your personal life as well as in the life of others. Delgado, Bernal, and Solórzano (2001) assert that educators of students in urban areas also have an obligation to cultivate transformational resistance. We must provide strategies for students to be able to challenge anti-affirmative action, anti-bilingual education, anti-immigrant, and heterosexist legislation and polices. This is crucial to counteracting the results of ineffective, inappropriate, and often racist and sexist educational practices and policies that continue to fail many students of color.

THE CONSEQUENCES OF UNHOOKING

My approach to race relations changed after I enrolled in the master's program at the University of Utah. It was the professors in the department who provided me with a framework where I began criticizing the system and how it was problematic for me to be critical of the students. If I am truly going to be an advocate for students, students of color in particular, I am going to have to critique liberalism and recognize the experiences that my students bring to classroom. It was through this framework that my pedagogy changed. I began teaching students how to fight within the system (transformative resistance) and be critical of their oppression, even if it is hidden behind equality and universality. Recognizing the difficulty in the task, my belief is grounded firmly in "If a person does not stand for something then the person will fall for anything."

However, as a result, unhooking has a very violent turn in the form of what I refer to as "academic lynching." For the purposes of this chapter, I will use Juárez and Hayes' (In-Press) definition of academic lynching. We define academic lynching as a form of domestic terrorism in which individuals apply institutional power through e-mail correspondence, course evaluations, letters destined for personnel files, and other forms of official and unofficial actions, policies, and decisions as part of processes of White racial domination used to define those outside the realm.

Put plainly, these systems help to support and maintain White supremacy with the violence of domestic terrorism directed against those seen as threats to the historical privileging of Whiteness. Institutions and social systems, in turn, do not readily change or move toward more democratic and humanized forms of organization because domestic terrorism is readily and abundantly applied against any efforts by individuals or groups to resist or challenge White supremacy.

This unhooking from Whiteness has moved me from conformist resistance to transformative resistance. Individuals whose identity is framed in transformation are critical of the oppression and have a desire for social justice. I began to hold an awareness and critique of their oppressive conditions and the structures of domination. Now, this critique does not come at a cost, as I have argued at the outset of this section, and for me that cost comes in the form of academic lynching, especially now that I have moved into teacher education.

When I moved into higher education, at an institution that prides itself on being progressive and has social justice in their mission statement, I quickly found out it was a bad idea to question my White colleagues about cultural diversity and poverty issues. When I began to question racist practices in the program, the violence began. I was called a Black Supremacist. My colleagues were caught up in ideology versus research around these issues: now, I recognize my approach should have been a little less aggressive. However, I had unhooked myself from placating Whiteness prior to coming into higher education, and I was not going to regress.

When I arrived in higher education, my department was using the racist text by Ruby Payne. While I knew the racist historical context of this book, I began to question the use of this text. My academic lynching began when I simply asked a question.

"Why is there a modification for poverty on the lesson plan form?" I asked, adding, "My fear is that teachers will lower their expectations for students who come from lower socioeconomic groups." When I asked the question, the work of Kozol (1991) and Macleod (1997) came to mind, so I knew that the lowering of expectations happens based on social class.

"That will not happen," my colleague Michelle[1] replied. I, however, had already heard teacher candidates in the class make negative comments about children from homes impacted by poverty and how they would not hold the same high expectations for students who come from lower socioeconomic situations as for students who come from economically privileged backgrounds.

I was hoping that my ideas and comments would provide a counter-argument to Ruby Payne's (1998) book, *A Framework for Understanding Poverty*, which is the foundational text in the diversity class. I was shocked by her reaction. She immediately silenced me. I expected my question to spark a dialogue not a tongue-lashing.

This was the first instance of where I became a victim of academic lynching. This faculty member prided herself on being such a progressive. Michelle stood up and proceeded to tell me why, based on her own personal experiences growing up in poverty and having had experiences similar to those described by Payne (1998), race was not an important factor to consider for teaching, let alone for social justice. It was not about race, she said, it was about class. Validating her experiences as more important and legitimate than mine and discrediting my experiences and the research in the field, Michelle came to my office and told me not to come back to her class. I was not welcome to shadow her any further; a second instance of being a victim of the brutality of Whiteness and my attempt to challenge it.

The week after Thanksgiving break, I was asked to meet with the department chair. I immediately knew something was wrong, just from prior experience dealing with management when I was a public school teacher. I wanted to find someone to go into the meeting with, but as a new faculty member I did not know who I could ask, and I was advised against contacting an attorney or Human Resources. Hindsight is 20/20 and the next time something like this happens, I will be more prepared, but I went into the meeting alone. When I went into the department chair's office, I was presented with a letter and was informed that he had already contacted Human Resources. I am not going to recreate the letter but only present the important sections that illustrate how the structure of the department showed its Whiteness. Statements from the letter are in italics followed by my reaction.

The letter started off with *given the reports I have received from a number of sources, including faculty whose judgment and observations I trust and students, regarding your performance to date. From all of the reports that I have received, the shadowing² process has not seemed to work well for you. You have tended to treat the class in a very causal manner in term of both your presence and your attitude. You have interrupted class to argue with the instructor regarding instructional resources and pedagogy. Comments from students related to your behavior in classes in which you shadow include "indifferent," "rude," and "hostile."*

The words "indifferent," "rude," "hostile," "showing arrogance" and "offhand behavior" can be classified as racial micro-aggressions. These terms, the verbal nooses used to hang faculty of color, are used as a way to control people of color in academia who may have a different research agenda or are outspoken about issues of equality and access. The department chair did remind me that I am on probation for the next three years.

The problem statement in this portion of the reprimand is *willingness to develop professionally in the direction that we need you to go.* After much thought about that statement, I had to ask myself exactly what did that mean? I am at an institution of higher learning that has a policy of academic freedom. There was no formal induction process that outlined "my direction," and because I have my own direction, now I was being reprimanded for it. It did not make sense to me. I can only interpret this as "Cleveland, you need to be a well-behaved Negro and conform to our expectations."

HOW I UNHOOKED: A CRITICAL RACE THEORETICAL PERSPECTIVE

In this section, using the tenets of CRT, I explain what I have learned over the years about beginning the process of unhooking from Whiteness, noting that I still have a lot to learn in the process about unhooking. The question for me, then, becomes how do I move this from the Ivory Tower of Academia into a grassroots movement in hopes of making it "better" for the next generation?

First, I had to learn and accept that racism is an endemic part of American society. Not the aggressive forms of racism but the subtle forms of racism that come in the forms of micro-aggressions or in having a White person tell me that I am really not Black as if it were a compliment rather than an insult. I also have to realize that when people hooked to Whiteness refuse to consider the everyday realities of race and racism, it is because this self-reflection requires them to face their own racist behavior and to name the contours of racism, and to realize it is less about them and more about Whiteness (Bergerson, 2003; Dei, Karumanchery and Karumanchery-Luik; 2007; Gillborn, 2005). Indeed, Whiteness silences any discussion of race outside of niceties of liking people who look like the racial other.

Second, I had to learn that there is no such thing as true colorblindness; in fact, colorblindness is not an appropriate ideal for social justice. According to Bergerson (2003), Whites attribute negative stereotypes to people of color while at the same time espousing their opposition to blatant racism. When White liberals fail to understand how they can and do embody White supremacist values even though they themselves may not embrace racism, through this lack of awareness they support the racist domination they wish to eradicate (Gillborn, 2005; hooks, 1989).

Tim Wise (2008) argues that colorblindness leads to even deeper systematic racism. The key word in Wise's statement is *systematic* racism. Something that scholars who study Whiteness realize when they begin to pull back the layers is that Whiteness never addresses the institution as racist. Critical Race Theory Scholars (Crits) argue that holding onto a colorblind framework only allows these *Friends* to address the egregious forms of racism, the ones everyone would notice and condemn, such as a White person calling an African American the "N" word in public. Yet, because racism is embedded in our thought processes and social structures, the ordinary business in our society keeps people of color in subordinate positions through daily interactions and practices. Only aggressive, color-conscious efforts to change the way things are done will do much to ameliorate misery inflicted on people of color by White racism (Delgado & Stefancic, 2001; Tate, 1997).

My academic lynching serves to protect the existing racial hierarchy in education and society because those deemed respectable and professional are the nice people

27

who use their abilities to draw on institutional power to silence those deemed as disrespectful within the context of White supremacy. Importantly, Whiteness defines the normative standards of what is considered respectful. Therefore, being respectful within the context of White supremacy necessarily means collusion with and perpetuation of the historical privileging of Whiteness.

Third, I had to understand that merit is problematic in the United States. It is not enough to say that anyone who works hard can achieve success. Students of color are systematically excluded from education and educational opportunities despite their hard work. Merit operates under the burden of racism; racism thus limits the applicability of merit to people of color (Bergerson, 2003). The hard work of some pays off much more than the hard work of racial others. Being passed over for the Assistant Hall Director after all my hard work, I remained invisible within my work contexts even though at that time I was not disrupting Whiteness and should not have become a target of Whiteness. My hard work was not valued by the official discourses of the institutions where I worked.

Next, I had to learn the role that my experiential knowledge as a Black man and the stories of other people of color, namely my Black and Brown students, play in their discourses. Angela Valenzuela's (1999) book *Subtractive Schooling,* which I read in my Ph.D. studies, opened my eyes to understanding how important these experiences are. As someone who was employing Whiteness, I was oftentimes unwilling to recognize the knowledge of those who are victims of the brutality of Whiteness as legitimate, appropriate, and critical to us (my students and me) as we were trying to navigate in a society grounded in racial subordination.

What I began to understand is that Whiteness is usually postured toward faculty members of color and students of color who refuse to remain silenced and to be the well-behaved minority (Hayes & Juárez, 2009; Juárez & Hayes, 2010). This is what Hytten and Warren (2003) call appeals to authenticity. In their model, when people hooked to Whiteness cited their experiences to counter or contradict non-White voices, their experiences were usually a means to undermine others experiences. An example of academic lynching would be a White professor standing in class espousing his/her majoritarian story as a non-majoritarian story; he/she is using his/her experiences as a weapon to silence. This is the same academic lynching that students of color face from teachers who subscribe to Whiteness and who do not value the experiences their students bring to the classroom; I was one of those teachers. Remember, Whiteness is not about skin color. I contend that during this journey my silence along with trying to protect my students from this violence not only did not prevent further violence; it was also an act of violence. When I was teaching in silence while my students were protecting themselves from this violence by exercising transformative resistance, this left my students labeled as the angry and disruptive ones (self-defeating resistance). Now that I am on this journey from Whiteness, I inform the pre-service teachers that I work with that in order to minimize conflict in the classroom, you as the teacher must recognize the experiences that their students bring to the classroom and draw on those experiences.

Most importantly, I had to learn about a type of "clan" mentality that continues to create a divide between Whites and people of color. Specifically, "clan" is the basic unit of all social organization. Following Maslow's theory of needs, "social belongingness" is a deficiency need, which means it is something we require in order to meet higher needs, and so take more or less for granted once it is met. Unlike higher order needs, social belongingness is not something we want to keep working at acquiring. For that matter, the signifiers for belonging are mostly non-verbal, pre-conscious. In the American context, skin tone is a potent signifier for who belongs "where" and "to whom".

So out of this clan mentality, this binary construction around race—the surface, economic realities and the sub-surface psychosexual dimensions—has served a very potent and effective means for distracting White "consciousness" from ever confronting "the man." In other words, Whites, out of fear of losing the privilege associated with being White, will stand on the sidelines and watch social injustices rather than speak out against them (Leonardo, 2009). Importantly, the expectation is that Whites are supposed to remain united even when they disagree with other Whites. A group of people who line up behind the rhetoric of individuality, working hard, not complaining, etc. will join that group around Whiteness. Because of this same Whiteness when given the choice to do what is right versus what is White, the White choice is the one chosen. This has probably been the hardest realization on my journey away from Whiteness: the realization that there is no such discourse as meritocracy and working hard, because no matter how hard I work, I will never be White or have the benefits that come along with being White.

IT HAS NOT BEEN EASY

I began resisting the stereotype that Black boys were incapable of succeeding in college prep classes. Sanders (1997) describes how many Black students respond to the necessity of being superior by not being superior. She explains, "Many African American students have mentally withdrawn from schooling as a response to the occupational and educational discrimination" (p. 83). I was determined that I was not going to be one of those students. I was mentally aware of my oppression, I thought, but I was not critical of it. As I described in my portrait, providing a critique of White racism was not part of my identity. I had to prove myself superior, which meant placing a distance between myself and those Blacks I felt did not display the characteristics that Whiteness wanted. Sanders (1997) would describe my behavior as "overproving" myself. She states that many African American students are forced to prove their equality by being superior. This needing to be superior is a response by many African American students to the fact that racism is an endemic part of American society.

This response to racism by being superior causes Black students as well as Black teachers to cross epistemological boundaries. In terms of Black students, many give up their sense of identity and their indigenous cultural system in order to achieve success as defined in a dominant group's terms, resulting in the notion of racelessness (Fordham, 1988; Sanders, 1997). But at the end of the day it did not matter how hard I worked, how much distance I put between myself and Blackness and valued Whiteness, how hard I worked to be "White-like"; I was never going to be White and enjoy the privileges that go along with being White. I had to learn the hard way that this talk of individuality and working hard was just White rhetoric to keep other Blacks at odds with each other. I should have known. Whiteness has a history of this, for instance, by creating divisions between house slaves and field slaves. These notions of individuality also keep persons of color at odds with each other; DuBois (1969) describes in *Back Toward Slavery* how powerful Whites convinced poor Whites that although they may not have material property they had Whiteness as property, and we see it with the division between Black, Brown, and Yellow folk. One day, I woke up and decided, like Nicholas Hartlep (see his chapter in this volume), that I too will no longer be a pawn of Whiteness. I learned that there is no compromising with Whiteness, which has been one of my hardest lessons.

NOTES

[1] Michelle is the faculty member whom I was shadowing. Michelle is not the professor's real name.
[2] At this University, before a faculty member can teach a class he/she has to shadow a professor who has taught the class. In my opinion, this shadowing process only serves as a way to continue the oppressive hegemonic practices of the department.

REFERENCES

Bergerson, A. A. (2003). Critical race theory and white racism: Is there room for White scholars in fighting racism in education? *Qualitative Studies in Education, 16*(1), 51–63.

Bonilla-Silva, E. (2010). *Racism with racists: Color-blind racism & racial inequality in contemporary America*. Lanham, MD: Rowman & Littlefield.

Delgado, R. (1989). Storytelling for oppositionists and others: A plea for narrative. *Michigan Law Review, 87*(8), 2411–2441.

Delgado, R., & Stefancic, J. (2001). *Critical race theory: An introduction*. New York: University Press.

Delgado Bernal, D., & Solorzano, D. (2001). Examining transformational resistance through a critical race and LatCrit theory framework: Chicana and Chicano students in an urban contex. *Urban Education, 36*(3).

Dei, G. J. S., Karumanchery, L. L., & Karumanchery-Luik, N. (2007). *Playing the race card: Exposing White power and privilege*. New York, NY: Peter Lang.

DuBois, W. E. B. (1969). *The souls of black folk*. New York: New American Library.

Fairbanks, C. (1996). Telling stories: Reading and writing research narratives. *Journal of Curriculum and Supervision, 11*, 320–340.

Fordham, S. (1996). *Blacked out: Dilemmas of race, identity and success at capital high*. Chicago: The University of Chicago Press.

Fordham, S. (1988). Racelessness as a factor in the black students' school success: Pragmatic strategy or pyrrhic victory? *Harvard Educational Review, 58*(1), 54–83.

Frankenberg, R. (1993). *White women, race matters: The social construction of Whiteness*. Minneapolis: University of Minnesota Press.

Gillborn, D. (2005). Education policy as an act of white supremacy: Whiteness, critical race theory and education reform. *Journal of Education Policy, 20*(4), 485–505.

Harris, C. (1995). Whiteness as property. In K. Crenshaw, N. Gotanda, G. Peller, & K. Thomas (Eds.) *Critical race theory: The key writings that formed the movement* (pp. 276–291). New York: The New Press.

Hartlep, N. D. (2010). *Going public: Critical race theory and issues of social justice.* Mustang, OK: Tate.

Hayes, C., & Juárez, B. G. (2009). You showed your Whiteness: You don't get a good white people medal. *International Journal of Qualitative Studies in Education, 22*(6), 729–744.

hooks, b. (1989). *Talking back: Thinking feminist, thinking black.* Boston, MA: South End Press.

Hytten, K., & Warren, J. (2003). Engaging Whiteness: how racial power gets reified in education. *International Journal of Qualitative Studies in Education, 16*(1), 65–89.

Juárez, B. G., & Hayes, C. (In-Press). Too black, yet not black enough: Challenging white supremacy in US Teacher Education and the making of radical social misfits. In F. Briscoe & M. Khalifa, (Eds.) *Becoming critical: Oppression, resistance and the emergence of a critical educator/researcher.* New York: SUNY Press.

Juárez, B. G., & Hayes, C. (2010). Social justice is not spoken here: Considering the nexus of knowledge, power, and the education of future teachers in the United States, *Power and Education, 2*(3), 233–252.

Kendall, F. E. (2006). *Understanding white privilege: Creating pathways to authentic relationships across race.* New York, NY: Routledge.

Knaus, C. B. (2009). Shut up and listen: Applied critical race theory in the classroom. *Race Ethnicity and Education, 12*(2), 133–154.

Kohli, R. (2009). Critical race reflections: valuing the experiences of teachers of color in teacher education. *Race Ethnicity and Education, 12*(2), 235–251.

Kozol, J. (1991). *Savage inequalities.* New York, NY: Crown Publishers.

Ladson-Billings, G. (1998). Just what is critical race theory and what is it doing in a nice field like education? *International Journal of Qualitative Studies in Education, 11*(1), 7–24.

Leonardo, Z. (2010). *Race, Whiteness and education.* New York, NY: Routledge.

MacLeod, J. (1997). *Ain't no makin' it: Aspirations and attainment in a low income neighborhood.* San Francisco, CA: Westview Press.

McCray, A., Sindelar, P., Kilgore, K., & Neal, L. (2002). African American women's decisions to become teachers: Sociocultural perspectives. *Qualitative Studies in Education, 15*(3), 269–290.

Parker, L., & Lynn, M. (2002). What's race got to do with it? Critical Race Theory's conflicts with and connections to qualitative research methodology and epistemology. *Qualitative Inquiry, 8*(1), 23–44.

Payne, R. K. (1998). *A framework for understanding poverty.* (3rd revised edition). Highlands, TX: Aha! Process, Inc.

Reed-Danahy, D. E. (1997). *Auto/Ethnography: Rewriting the self and the social.* New York, NY: Oxford University Press.

Sanders, M. G (1997). Overcoming obstacles: Academic achievement as a response to racism and discrimination. *The Journal of Negro Education, 66*(1), 83–93.

Sleeter, C., & Delgago Bernal, D. (2002). Critical pedagogy, critical race theory, and antiracist education: Implications for multicultural education. In J. A. Banks & C. A. Banks (Eds.) *Handbook of research on multicultural education* (2nd ed.). San Francisco, CA: Jossey Bass.

Valenzuela, A. (1999). *Subtractive schooling.* New York: State University of New York Press.

Tate, W. F. (1997). Critical race theory and education: History, theory, and implications. *Review of Research in Education, 22*, 195–247.

Wise, T. (2008). *Speaking treason fluently: Anti-racist reflections from an angry white male.* New York: Soft Skull Press.

BRENDA JUÁREZ

3. LEARNING TO TAKE THE BULLET AND MORE

*Anti-racism Requirements for White Allies and Other Friends
of the Race, So-Called and Otherwise*

WHAT'S A WHITE PERSON TO DO?
INQUIRING ABOUT WHITENESS, RACE, AND SOCIAL JUSTICE

Not long ago I received an e-mail from someone I did not know—we'll call her Sara. Sara was in earnest; she was searching for answers and she wanted those answers from me.

Taken off guard, I wasn't sure I had any answers for Sara. What could I say to her? What *should* I say to her? My mind began racing, searching frantically for something, for anything, that might be of use toward composing some kind of an answer.

I sat back to ponder Sara's questions. Like the sincere young White woman who once approached Malcolm X asking the same questions (Cone, 2004), Sara wanted to know, "What, if anything, can those White people of goodwill do in struggles toward social justice? What is the role of sincere White people in social justice endeavors?"

Sara's questions are profoundly important to matters of humanity, the world, and a society like our own in the U.S. that aspires to democratic ideals. There are very real, very material consequences for the ways we answer Sara's questions. The answers to Sara's questions drive the ways we make sense of and act on the social injustices that surround us in our communities and around the globe.

Thinking about Sara's questions and how I should approach putting together some kind of answer, given the significance of the topic, I began to feel some anger toward Sara and her request for information—as if it was so easy and straightforward to give some kind of no-bake, no-cook, instantly ready recipe-formula on how to undo centuries of White racial oppression. The topic Sara was inquiring about is enormous and deeply complex—what did she expect me to do? Did Sara really think that it was such a simple matter of just hitting the reply button, typing up a few sentences in a kind of check-list format, and then five minutes later clicking the send button? Was I really expected to fit an explanation of a topic this size into an e-mail reply? Ridiculous. Outrageous.

Yet, taking a deep breath, I recognized that Sara was not the one I should feel anger toward; she, like the rest of us, had inherited the existing unequal conditions

*C. Hayes and N.D. Hartlep (Eds.), Unhooking from Whiteness:
The Key to Dismantling Racism in the United States, 33–51.*
© *2013 Sense Publishers. All Rights Reserved.*

of society. She had also inherited her place within society's unequal conditions as a White person living within a social context organized to reflect and privilege the interests of White people and therefore not required to "see" race-based inequities.

In the U.S., particularly among White people, Sara included, some of us hope—and far more of us assume—that we have already arrived at true equality and social justice in our society despite unending evidence to the contrary everywhere around us. "The record is there for all to read. It resounds all over the world. It might as well be written in the sky" as James Baldwin (1985) once observed (p. 410). Unfortunately, as the Black American folk aphorism goes (Mills, 1997), when White people say *Justice*, they mean *just us*. Sara's questions reflected what seemed to be her recent discovery that the world around her was not the landscape of equality she had always been taught to presume it was.

WHO IS A FRIEND OF FREEDOM?
CAN WHITE PEOPLE BE ALLIES FOR SOCIAL JUSTICE?

In this chapter, I attempt to begin answering Sara's questions, albeit quite tentatively. With Lerone Bennett Jr. (1964), I explore "Who is [and is not] freedom's friend?" (p. 77). I consider, specifically, the topic of White people of goodwill as [un]reliable allies in struggles toward social justice by seeking to address a few questions of my own. Can White people be allies for social justice, for example? What is a White ally? How will we recognize a White ally if we meet one? How would an individual who is White become a White ally? And, most importantly, why is it that in the U.S., a nation supposedly founded on egalitarian principles, there have been so few White people who have been [reliable] allies in struggles for social justice?

I begin by linking Sara's questions to historical traditions of social justice and race relations in the U.S. considering the history of anti-racism among Whites in the U.S. Drawing on my own personal and professional experiences as a White, female teacher educator seeking to help push forward social justice, I situate Sara's struggle for understanding of Whites' role in social justice within the context of multicultural teacher education and my own struggles for understanding. I then examine some ways of defining what it means to be a White ally, and I consider how I have attempted to work against Whiteness in my own personal and professional lives while working toward enacting a kind of White antiracist praxis for social justice as I have attempted to create and live it.

Whiteness, pointedly, refers to the historical and systemic privileging of the interests, values, beliefs, accomplishments, and histories of White people as a group (Gillborn, 2005). Grounded in Whiteness, White supremacy is defined as "a racialized social system that upholds, reifies, and reinforces the superiority of whites" (Leonardo, 2005, p. 127). White people of goodwill, in turn, are identified as those individuals who self-identify and are identifiable as White and hold positive feelings and intentions of goodwill toward historically stigmatized social groups and oppose acts of coercion and race hate and any form of inequality (Frankenberg, 1997). White supremacy is [re]created through processes of race-based domination as Whites collectively and individually, regardless of intentions, and sometimes supported by people of color, make decisions, interact, and act in ways that help to maintain and further the historical privileging of Whiteness (Feagin, 2010; Leonardo, 2005).

HOW DOES IT FEEL TO BE A WHITE PROBLEM? THE PROBLEM OF WHITE PEOPLE OF GOODWILL AND WHITE ANTIRACISM

Contrary to the beliefs of some, White people as a group do not hold a very compelling or positive track record when it comes to issues of social justice; within nearly every domain of U.S. society, White people retain supremacy (Aptheker, 1993). Collectively, rather, Whites have worked hard to maintain their supremacy in U.S. society by working to derail and sabotage social justice endeavors (Painter, 2010).

Take as one representative example, if you will, the situation of the White people of goodwill in Alabama during the 1960's struggles and the role they took up and enacted during the street demonstrations of those seeking social justice at the time. Inspiring the now famous letter written in 1963 from within the Birmingham jail in Alabama, the eight White clergymen who publically criticized the Reverend Dr. Martin Luther King Jr. for his refusal to stop the street demonstrations in Birmingham, Alabama represented other White people of goodwill making up the White church in the American South, including rabbis, ministers, and priests. These White people of goodwill, officially dedicated to egalitarian principles espoused by their Judeo-Christian theologies, were for all intents and purposes—at least on the surface—in favor of ideas such as the brotherhood of all men as the children of God and the notion that God loves all of His children equally. Notwithstanding, of those White people of goodwill whom King felt should have been his strongest allies in the fight for social justice, "some have been outright opponents, refusing to understand the freedom movement and misrepresenting its leaders; all too many have been more cautious than courageous and have remained silent behind the anesthetizing security of stained-glass windows..." (King, 1964, p. 19).

Could any of these White people of goodwill be considered allies in the struggle for social justice, then? Probably not. The biggest barrier to social justice, as King pointed out (1964), is—unfortunately—usually a problem of good, that is to say, a problem of sincere White people of goodwill and their *shallow understanding* and *lukewarm acceptance*, not *the outright rejection* of White or any other people of ill will. If we take the example of the eight clergymen in Alabama as representative of general patterns of activity among White people of goodwill, and I believe that we can given the evidence put forth by the historical record of antiracism in the US—Sara's questions about White people and social justice therefore take on a particularly pointed significance for struggles toward social equality today. Race- based disparities remain durably embedded across U.S. society and the world and are reflected by profound disparities between Whites and people of color in contemporary domains of healthcare, employment, educational attainment levels, rates of incarceration, and more.

Yet, when asked "Who is freedom's friend?" (Bennett, 1964), Whites as a group, and as a general rule, still tend to find this question particularly obtuse because the answer is blatantly, even embarrassingly (for you if you do not see it this way) obvious—"We are!" The "we" here does refer to White people, a point that is underscored by the notion of "all-American" which in the U.S. most assuredly does not refer to African Americans, Native Americans, Arab Americans, Asian American, Mexican Americans or any other group of hyphenated Americans. Notably, people of color in the U.S. and around the globe have sometimes seen social justice matters quite differently in terms of White people as freedom's friend—enslaved Africans who crossed the Atlantic in chains, for example, or Native peoples who walked the Trail of Tears (and headed eastward, not westward), or our Japanese brothers and sisters sent to internment camps on American soil, or those lost at Hiroshima and Nagasaki, or others lost in the Philippines—and the list of atrocities at the hands of White people collectively goes on (Painter, 2010).

Sara's e-mailed queries, whether she was aware of it or not, thus directly tapped into a profoundly important and immensely contradictory tension within the history and fabric of U.S. society—the conflict-filled role of White people in struggles for social justice. Frederick Douglass (1845/2001), the great American Orator and Abolitionist, for instance, also struggled mightily with what to do about and how to manage with William Lloyd Garrison—a White person of goodwill who had his printing press destroyed and was almost lynched by other Whites for his abolitionist activities. Douglass eventually decided to establish his own newspaper apart from Garrison's newspaper when Garrison continued to act in patronizing ways that suggested he knew best and could and should speak for all enslaved and freed Africans and African Americans (Lester, 1968).

Interestingly, many of the White people of goodwill from the northern U.S. who were involved in abolitionist activities were more prepared to die for enslaved Black people than they were to live with them in their communities (Quarles, 1974). Lerone Bennett Jr. (1972) has noted the six strategies that African Americans have shifted back and forth between using in attempting to collectively collaborate with White people and to help African Americans to realize this sense of Whites' group identity as freedom's friend:

1) Blacks creating a coalition with the power structure represented by rich, upper-class Whites, for example, philanthropists, power brokers, and entrepreneurs; 2) Blacks seeking a coalition with middle-class White progressives or liberals more or less committed to the American creed; 3) Blacks working toward an alliance with relatively poor Whites in labor solidarity; 4) Blacks aligning with

radical Whites of the old and new Left; 5) Blacks collaborating with other minority and ethnic groups; and 6) Blacks organizing among themselves (see pp. 179–180).

Though Sara probably didn't know it at the time, her questions about Whiteness and social justice, as immensely important as they are, accordingly, are not new or unique to her, not now and not historically in the U.S. (King, 1996). People of color have been trying to get White people to actually be freedom's friend for quite some time now. It doesn't seem outrageous to conclude that there has been a lack of listening on the part of Whites about what it means to be freedom's friend from those who have been systemically denied freedom. Despite—and perhaps because of—the historical tenacity of Sara's questions, then, we must continue to seek answers to those questions regarding White people and struggles toward social justice in our own times and for ourselves in our particular contexts (Juárez & Hayes, 2012).

THE LIMITS OF GOODWILL AND WHITE SUPREMACY: AN OFTEN DIFFICULT MOMENT OF TRUTH FOR WHITE PEOPLE

The role of White people in social justice struggles throughout U.S. history has therefore been problematic and filled with contradictory tensions at best. Even [perhaps especially?] as a group sincere White people of goodwill have, over time, not been reliable friends of freedom with regard to people of color and struggles toward social justice. For this reason, it has usually been with a certain sense of irony, and tongue in cheek, that people of color have over time frequently referred to sincere White people of goodwill as *Friends of the Race* (Harris, 1992).

I'm thinking, for example, about how W. E. B. DuBois (1935, 1973) and Carter G. Woodson (1933/2000), among others, astutely noted that the education many of the helpers and *friends of the race* from the North and elsewhere after the Civil War were providing to Black children amounted, in reality, to a form of educational slavery (Harris, 1992). With plenty of warm feelings of racial goodwill to spread around, these so-called *friends of the race* were very effectively preparing Black children and youth to take their places as second class citizens within a supposedly democratic nation based on colorblind, race-neutral ideals of equality and justice.

The goodwill and good intentions of these sincere White people dedicated to democratic ideals has thus historically not been enough to overcome the tensions and paradoxes that their participation in social justice struggles has entailed. For the most part, indeed, the participation of White people of goodwill has been a mixed bag of benefits and limitations that has in many ways impeded instead of helped push forward the realization of social justice—to put it very kindly (Feagin, 2010; West, 1997).

To overcome this problematic past, then, it is important to understand how White people of goodwill have often helped to sustain White supremacy despite their good intentions. Sara's actions in contacting me reflect these historical tensions of

White people's conflicting and paradoxical roles in social justice struggles (Hayes & Juárez, 2009). Very importantly, Sara chose to contact me with her questions about Whiteness and social justice not because I happen to be some sort of expert White-ally know-it-all guru on White people and social justice struggles but because I, too, have struggled and continue to struggle over these very same questions regarding Whiteness, White people, and social justice (Hayes & Juárez, 2009).

Like Sara, I also happen to be a White woman who is also a teacher educator tasked with the assignment of preparing a mostly White, female, and primarily-English-speaking population of future teachers to successfully teach all students within today's socially diverse public schools. Although I had never met Sara or known of her before receiving her e-mail, it was no coincidence that she contacted me nor that there are so many similarities in our personal stories and professional backgrounds as White women who are teacher educators seeking social justice through the multicultural preparation of future teachers (Juárez & Hayes, 2010). In this nation, most teachers and teacher educators are White, and many of them are also women (Juárez, Smith, & Hayes, 2008). Sara contacted me at the recommendation of one of her colleagues, an African-American man who is a science educator—we'll call him Tyson.

Tyson's recommendation that Sara contact me is indicative of the particular struggles between the two of them to communicate across deeply historical divides as well as the difficulties that they faced in trying to figure out what it means to prepare White teachers to successfully teach students of color. Yet their negative experience of failed cross-racial attempts to communicate is not just their own unique set of frustrations but part of a patterned set of racial relations situated within and reflective of U.S. society's existing racial hierarchy (Hayes & Juárez, 2012). The frustrations Tyson and Sara have faced in trying to collaborate toward social justice across racial lines are instructive because they highlight some of the very reasons why White allies have been so few and far between throughout U.S. history. Any responses to Sara's inquiries about Whiteness and social justice cannot be fully explored without some understanding of why it has been outside the norm for White people to have any productive involvement in social justice endeavors.

Tyson had suggested that Sara get in touch with me after yet another one of their conversations about social justice in teacher education ended as they usually did: with both of them feeling completely frustrated and stuck in their efforts to collaborate across racial lines. Importantly, the historical record suggests that people of color teaching White people about their Whiteness has never been a particularly productive, fulfilling, or successful task assigned to people of color; people of color teaching White people about race and racism is quite like victims of rape trying to teach their victimizers about why rape is morally wrong and they should not do it, to put it quite bluntly (Hayes & Juárez, 2009; Juárez & Hayes, 2010). An alternative approach to teaching Whites about Whiteness and social justice is to have White people teach other White people.

Since Tyson happens to know me very well, being a long-time and close friend he hoped that I, as a White person myself, would be able to find a way to reach Sara and explain to her what he had worn himself out in trying to explain; that until White people (myself and Sara included) learn to address their Whiteness—all of their good intentions notwithstanding—they will continue to do what most well-intentioned White liberals have done in the past and continue to do: unwittingly affirm the maintenance and perpetuation of White supremacy. As bell hooks (1989) has explained,

> When liberal whites fail to understand how they can and/or do embody white-supremacist values and beliefs even though they may not embrace racism as prejudice or domination (especially domination that involves coercive control), they cannot recognize the ways their actions support and affirm the very structure of racist domination and oppression that they profess to wish to see eradicated (p. 113).

Race-based domination, then, is most consistently perpetuated by nice people, not hateful people, many of whom are professionals working in helping professions—teachers, police officers, healthcare providers, and so on (Juárez & Hayes, 2012). This point about White people of goodwill playing a central role in the perpetuation of White supremacy is a barrier that usually sifts out the White people of goodwill who want to remain in the role of the eight White clergymen in Alabama during the 1960s from those who like, John Brown, the White person who had such commitment to liberty and freedom-for-all that he went to the gallows for those ideals, are willing to put their lives on the line to challenge and push toward breaking down White supremacy.

Which type of White person of goodwill was Sara willing and ready to be? A sincere White person willing, like the eight clergymen in Alabama, to sit on the sidelines and look out at inequities suffered by people of color? A sincere White person like John Brown who was willing to, and did, die for the cause of social justice and freedom for all? As I see it, this is the crux of the issue that Tyson was trying to get Sara to confront. This was the moment of truth that seemed to be getting in the way of an effective cross-racial collaboration with Tyson—would Sara take up the challenge of facing the key role White people of goodwill play in perpetuating White supremacy? And thus I entered this conversation about White allies and other such [so-called] Friends of the Race.

Pointedly, I do not necessarily believe that it is an oxymoron for a person to be simultaneously White and dedicated to social justice. However—and this is very important—with J. O. Killens (1965), "I [also] know that there are White folk who want America to be the land of the free and the home of the brave, but there are far too few of them, and many of them are rarely brave" (p. 28). Regarding Whiteness and social justice—the truth be told—and with Richard Wright (1957), "I'm convinced that we all, deep in our hearts, know exactly what to do, though most of us would rather die than do it" (p. xvi). A moment of truth emerges for White people of goodwill when they must decide if they are willing to face and do something about the role of good intentions in sustaining White supremacy.

But what is it that White people of goodwill must do to face up to this challenge of the limitations of their goodwill and their good intentions—even if we all do already know deep in our hearts what we must do (Wright, 1957)? One would hope that the need for giving up one's life literally would be behind us in the U.S., but we can never presume this to be the case given U.S. and world history. Accordingly, let us make it explicit that which White people of goodwill must do to be freedom's actual friend. I draw on the Black American radical tradition to help me outline the anti-racism requirements for White people of goodwill who would be White anti-racist allies seeking to help push forward and realize social justice and freedom for all.

WHITE ALLIES: SINCERE WHITE PEOPLE AND MOVING BEYOND GOODWILL AND GOOD INTENTIONS

To paraphrase Malcolm X (Breitman, 1964), if you are not willing to die for freedom, take the word out of your vocabulary. This willingness to put your life on the line for freedom, very significantly, is precisely that which distinguishes some White people of goodwill from others in terms of those sincere people who are White and working against rather than for White supremacy regardless of their intentions and goodwill. The answer as to what White people can do to participate in social justice struggles is deceptively simple—they must be "willing to die to overcome the suffering of people of color—and thereby secure freedom for all of us" (West, 1993, p. 178). James Baldwin (1985) argued that a sincere person who is White must consent "… in effect, to become black himself [or herself], to become part of that suffering and dancing country that [s]he now watches wistfully from the heights of his lonely power and, armed with spiritual traveler's checks, visits surreptitiously after dark" (p. 375). Very directly, as a friend explained it to me: "You must be willing to take the bullet for me."

Lest I be interpreted here as being overly melodramatic and unrealistic, please allow me to elaborate on what I mean when I suggest that it is necessary for a person who is White to become Black and to be willing to take the bullet for people of color. I'm using the term Black here in a kind of metaphorical sense. The notion of race itself is a socially constructed matter, that is, an invention created by White people, which continues to have very real and very violently limiting consequences for the lives and life chances of people of color. Thus, one is not born White or Black; one must learn to be White; one must learn to be Black, and so on.

Moreover, as Malcolm X also came to understand later in his life—a life that was much, much too short—being White is more about using a certain mindset to make sense of and act in the world around you than it is about the amount of melanin that is reflected in your skin color. Of course, I can never completely disassociate myself from being the recipient of benefits that have historically accrued to the incident of being born into and thus raised as a member of Whites as a racial group given

40

that because of the lightness of the color of my skin I am identified and identifiable as a White person. Neither am I talking about becoming Black in the sense of changing the tone of my skin color or my hair texture or style or the cadences of my spoken language or anything else associated with the cultural practices of being Black— although there are several quite humorous books written by Black authors that engage for White people the topic of *How to be Black* (Thurston, 2012).

Instead, I am referring to becoming Black in the sense that you live your life in such a way that you cause such a ruckus in fighting against policies and programs and all else that support and help to recreate White supremacy that other White people either begin to make changes or push you out of the scene. When I say that I expect White allies to become Black, I follow Baldwin (1985) in saying that these sincere White people of goodwill must take on a way of thinking and operating within the world that constantly accounts for the continuing existence of White supremacy and its consequences on the lives of people of color, while keeping at the center of their thinking the incredible creativity and resiliency applied toward realizing justice for themselves despite the terrors of White supremacy. To do so, in turn, requires these sincere White people of goodwill to study in great detail the sweeping range of values, beliefs, interests, histories, and accomplishments of people of color that have heretofore been submerged and rendered invisible to them by the historical privileging of Whiteness.

Becoming an ally requires a White person to adopt a way of living, an orientation to life, not a specific tactic or practice apart from your daily business of living. It is to adopt a perspective from which you guide your actions and which is centrally grounded in continuously disrupting Whiteness and moving toward freedom—not something you do on the weekends at marches after you have finished activities in your other life. I am being intentionally specific here when I refer to needing to disrupt Whiteness to move toward freedom rather than equality, for example. Only White people as a group have had troubles with understanding that all people are already and always have been equal; people of color have historically taken this point as presumed and therefore have not needed to be convinced that they are equal to Whites.

The struggle against Whiteness is therefore, as Malcolm X eloquently stated on more than one occasion, about freedom to live as humans in this society—it is not about integration or segregation. Importantly, it is not about eradicating racial animus and changing the negative attitudes of White people toward acceptance of all peoples. With James Cone (2004) on matters of racial attitudes applied to gender issues, for instance, I am not particularly interested in people's attitudes toward me as a woman—be they attitudes negative, positive, or otherwise toward gender— unless [and this is a very big unless] these people with their negative attitudes toward women have the institutional authority to make decisions based on their anti-woman attitudes, which then serve to constrain the opportunities and conditions of my life in ways that inhibit my ability to pursue my own interests and aims.

Given what I have just described as what it takes to be a White ally, it is perhaps not terribly surprising that there have been so few reliable White allies throughout

U.S. history—most of us seem to be much too comfortable with tending to our own comforts while not realizing that if one side of our society goes down, the rest of us are going down as well; our destinies are intertwined.

Indeed, as Malcolm X would frequently quip—and I am paraphrasing here—if you aren't seriously disrupting things, you probably aren't saying much. Ture and Hamilton (1967) put it this way:

> Jobs will have to be sacrificed, positions of prestige and status given up, favors forfeited. It may well be—and we think it is—that leadership and security are basically incompatible. When one forcefully challenges the racist system, one cannot at the same time, expect that system to reward him or even treat him comfortably (p. 15).

I find comfort in these words because in my life I have experienced to some degree these negative consequences, and I have fought hard not to internalize the punishments of the system of White supremacy enacted by its representatives in positions of authority in the institutions where I have worked, nor to accept my efforts to disrupt the system as deficiencies and shortcomings in me as they are officially defined.

For example, my teaching contract not being renewed—not officially because I fought against Whiteness and spoke truth to power, but instead, officially, because my teaching wasn't adequate. The official document reads,

> She knows a lot about cultural diversity and she is very outspoken…She receives some of the best student evaluations and some of the worst in the college and department. Consistent with past evaluations, students often couch a negative comment within an otherwise positive comment saying that the workload is heavy and that she uses 'shock and awe' techniques which include the use of profanity…. She has been advised to continue to evaluate her teaching practices to ensure that she meets the needs of all her students.[1]

I do recognize that this is a tall order, both in terms of the standards that sincere White people must reach in addressing Whiteness and social justice, and with regard to expecting them to give up job security and more; there are mortgages to be paid. Yet—and this is very significant—I had a mortgage to pay as well, and at the time I was a single mother with four teenagers to feed and clothe. More importantly, as I frequently would tell my students, the fact that I have a choice to decide whether or not I want to put my mortgage at risk is the very epitome of White privilege; people of color cannot get up in the morning and say to themselves, "Today is not a good day to be Black." or "I think I'll choose my White body because I'm too tired to deal with all the race-based discrimination that continuously and daily comes my way in my Black body and results in taking years off of my life." The life expectancy of African Americans is currently still at least six years less than that of White people (Washington, 2006).

Why should I or any other White person be excused from putting my mortgage and security on the line for freedom? Why should only people of color be expected to put everything on the line for freedom? As Dr. King put it (1964), *injustice anywhere is a threat to justice everywhere.*

Accordingly, I must ask myself: Am I like the many White liberals past and present who, as Bennett (1972) has described, want to tear off the cover of the book of White supremacy but keep the pages inside—have my cake and eat it too? Am I really about challenging White supremacy? Because if I am not, I join the many other sincere Whites who help to buttress rather than fight against the White supremacy they are supposedly against. My so-called help in struggles for social justice is more of a hindrance and barrier, then, if I am not willing to let those pages go, even tear them out as necessary.

At the same time, and very sincerely and humbly, I cannot say that I know myself to be at this standard of willingness to take the bullet from White supremacy literally when push comes to shove. Moreover, I would not dream of putting myself in the same category as John Brown, for example, who literally did die for the cause of freedom for all. In my own small way, however, I do believe that on a much lesser scale I have been pushed to decide just how much I would be willing to give up in terms of the privileges I enjoy from my Whiteness in order to disrupt White supremacy and to push harder toward social justice and freedom for all. What I can say, in other words, is that I do have some experience with instituting ruckus, enough to bring down the militant might and wrath of White supremacy on my head as reward for my efforts to disrupt it, as my colleagues and I have written about elsewhere (Juárez, Smith and Hayes, 2008; Juárez & Hayes, 2010). I do believe this is why Tyson suggested that Sara contact me.

Pointedly, as a person who is White and was born and raised surrounded almost completely by other White people within a context of overwhelming Whiteness isolated from people of color, I did not just wake up one day knowing that it was important for me to use my White privileges to work toward disrupting White supremacy and helping to push toward social justice for all. Indeed, my much loved and very inquisitive students in lower Alabama would get at this issue by repeatedly asking me, "What happened to you, Dr. J.?"

Implied within their questions, my teacher education students were asking me why I did not act like what they expected or had previously experienced from a White person. They weren't immediately comfortable with or sure how to respond to a White woman with long blonde hair, blue eyes, and a Malcolm X tattoo on her left upper arm, who inquired on the first day of class as to why it was that it in a city that was over half African-American there were so many White people in the room. I am always very serious about disrupting Whiteness from the very first day of class, and I never use velvet gloves to do so. Perhaps this is why I eventually caused such a ruckus that my contract was not renewed, and I was banished from my students there and had to take my family to another region of the country. White supremacy, enacted daily by those representatives of institutions who use their authority to make decisions that uphold the historical privileging of Whiteness, will tolerate only so much pushing back against the Whiteness of teacher education. I learned this the hard way, in a quest for courses on the history of Black education, for instance, at a public university located within the American Deep South

SHIFTING AWAY FROM WHITENESS: FACING THE CONSEQUENCES

I should note here that I am not very comfortable with the term White ally. I find the notion of being a White ally problematic because White supremacy, as I view it, is a White problem—White created and White sustained and perpetuated—and therefore not a "people of color problem." This is not to say, however, that I do not recognize that White supremacy fundamentally targets people of color, centrally and very violently influencing their lives and life chances. Because White supremacy is a White problem, then, I do not see Whites as allies to anything, but rather as responsible agents who need to get busy in dismantling this historical apparatus that we as a racial group have created over time. As I have often told my students, White people as a group have bloody hands.

Given my views on White supremacy and my unwillingness to use velvet gloves to approach the issue with other White, I have not always been terribly popular with other White people. Indeed, for me, the process of seeking to enact a lifestyle of anti-racism has been a process that has entailed a great deal of alienation, isolation, and rejection from other Whites including, most painfully, my family in terms of my parents and siblings. There have been times, for example, when I have called out the practice of telling racial jokes at parties (not unique to my family for sure) only to have members of my family tell me that I was over-reacting and had become a hater of my own kind. I am not now invited to most large family gatherings. My daily professional life, too, has been affected in many subtle yet important ways. Other professors who had never set foot in my classroom or had any conversations with me would advise my students—as my students would tell me—to stay away from my courses.

Yet my intent here is not to index the innumerable ways I have been pushed out by Whites because of my consistency in pointing out the Whiteness of my surroundings and for advocating more inclusive forms of participation and organization of settings. Indeed, anyone familiar with Whiteness, and the ways that White people are socialized from birth to make sense of the world in particular ways that privilege their interests, knows that as a group White people do not tolerate for long any deviation from these rules by other Whites without some type of castigation.

> "Again, the w\White groups tend to view their interests in a particularly united, solidified way when confronted with black demands which are seen as threatening to vested interests. The Whites react in a united group to protect interests they perceive to be theirs—interests possessed to the exclusion of those who, for varying reasons, are outside the group" (Ture & Hamilton, 1967, p. 7).

The White racial knowledge that White people tend to operationalize is a kind of knowing that is passed down across generations and is based on presumptions of Whites' moral superiority and the moral inferiority of people of color, thus rationalizing the supremacy of Whites in most domains of society (Smith, Jacobson, & Juárez, 2012; Picca & Feagin, 2007). White racial knowledge is different, then, from White people and what they individually know in terms of the assumptions about race they collectively use to interpret the world around them (Juárez & Hayes, 2012; Leonardo, 2005). Notably, people of color can and sometimes do enact White racial knowledge. However, people of color as individuals and groups do not have the institutional power to systemically enact their preferences, prejudices, biases, or applications of White racial knowledge.

At the same time, I do not wish to minimize the alienation and harms I have experienced as a result of speaking truth to power against White supremacy. It may seem to others at first glance that I am overly sensitive about these hurts; indeed, this is exactly what a member of my immediate family told me about my refusal to participate in the allowance of racial epithets expressed humorously or otherwise at all-White family dinner parties—I have been repeatedly told that I am over-reacting and being too politically correct about racial matters because no harm was intended and because I wouldn't accept that [White] people were just like that around these parts. No doubt it is true that White people in the area were "just like that" in terms of willingness to accept the continued perpetuation of assumptions about the moral and cultural inferiority of people of color. I was not willing to accept this response, however, because I know the reason why there were so few Black families in that area: Whites in the area where I grew up had consistently and systemically used violence to run Black families out of town. Moreover, White people in that area are still known for doing so. Given my resistance and unwillingness to participate in affirmations by White people of the inferiority of people of color, I was told that I was no longer welcome at my family's gatherings.

The personal rejections and professional punishments I received from other Whites because of my resistance do, when examined one at a time and outside of the patterned context of how regularly and how often I experienced them, initially appear to be matters of sensitivity, tolerance, and interpersonal relations gone bad. At the same time, I do not wish to paint myself as some long-suffering White person who has been abused by the race-hate of other Whites. In reality, though, these acts against me by other Whites were enacted to police me back into the normative ways of being, thinking, and knowing as a White person in ways that affirm and help to maintain the historical privileging of Whiteness. These acts by other Whites constitute micro-aggressions that in their isolated instances do not appear to do much harm apart from hurting my feelings—until the cumulative effect over time is examined. When each act of micro-aggression is linked systematically to other micro-aggressions, the harm done to the targeted individual is often pernicious; it manifests as severe economic harm, hampering one's ability to earn an income to maintain one's family and self; it may also create psychological harm, causing suffering that results in increased stress and depression; the impact of these and other cumulative effects may result in health problems that shorten one's life or limit one's life chances and experiences.

A TENTATIVE JOURNEY TOWARD ANTI-RACISM: BEING WHITE
AND LEARNING TO PUSH BACK AGAINST WHITENESS

Like most White people, I did not grow up thinking that I had to put myself and everything that I am and have on the line for equality, particularly given that I was born at the tail end of the Civil Rights era in the U.S. (Bonilla Silva, 203; Frankenberg, 1997). Rather, as a girl growing up on a farm in the American Midwest, I was taught tacitly and explicitly to view the world using White racial knowledge (Feagin, 2009). I grew up thinking, therefore, that this worldview was normal and thus not questioning that White people tended to be the ones in charge, the ones with authority and control in most institutions even when people of color made up the majority. I never once wondered as a child, for example, why it was that I lived in a town and attended a high school with an American Indian name and mascot, and yet never did I see any American Indian people anywhere around me in daily life. In fact, there were two large Indian reservations near my childhood home which no one—not my teachers, not my parents, no adults in my life—ever mentioned during my entire time growing up in the area. I never even saw a person of color until I was in the fourth grade, and it was such an exceptional incident that I remember it to this day.

Accordingly, I grew up having no idea about the atrocities inflicted on people of color through White supremacy by individuals and groups of White people who enacted processes of race-based domination (Leonardo, 2005)—there was a reason, I later learned, that I never heard about the American Indians or their land that I grew up on. When I would travel to larger cities and see what I did not then know were the symptoms of White supremacy in neighborhoods home to African Americans, I was still too inculcated with White racial knowledge to question the rationalizations I heard from the adults around me at the dinner table: that people of color were culturally and morally inferior to Whites. The negative stereotypes, images, narratives, and emotions I learned to associate with people of color surrounded me constantly as I grew up and became the basis for what I used to make sense of the world around me. I did not know at the time that I was seeing the consequences not the causes of poverty, sexism, racism, and other manifestations of White supremacy.

It wasn't until I moved away from the surroundings of my youth and later married a person of color that I began to question the assumptions of White racial knowledge that I had learned as a child. As a partner of a person of color, it wasn't long until I found myself in the shadows of the race-based discrimination that is constantly focused on people of color in U.S. society. My real education began when I became both a mother and a teacher of children who did not and could not pass as White. As I began to see my own young children and students take the bruising of White supremacy's assumptions of the inferiority of people of color, I began searching for answers as to why the world was not as racially equal or socially just as I, like Sara, had officially been taught to believe as a child.

My search brought me to graduate school and, thus, to the companionship of friends who were also graduate students and first generation college students like myself. The distinguishing factor between them, and me however, was that they were also students of color. Fortunately for me, both they and my professors were not shy about correcting me when my Whiteness was glaringly and embarrassingly showing regardless of my sincerity and goodwill—which was most of the time. It was during graduate school that I met Tyson and my other good friend who advised me that I had to be willing to take the bullet for him and other people of color if I was truly to live my life as an antiracist who sought to disrupt White supremacy. Under conditions of White supremacy, as Bennett (1964) has noted, friendship is an action not a pledge.

And this friend—we'll call him Dae'quan—was correct. It wasn't but a few months after graduation, hot out of grad school and into my first position as a teacher educator, that I was presented with my first opportunity to learn to take the bullet for Dae'quan. As the only Black man on the faculty and the only member of the faculty on a soft-money contract, Dae'quan was about to be fired from his job. Although no one said the two incidents were connected, it just so happened that Dae'quan was losing his job at the time that one of his publications on race and religion came out in press. The concurrence of the publication and his being ousted was, officially, a coincidence. However, with the local radio station and newspaper publicizing his writing, there were many White people in the area who viewed Dae'quan as being a Black supremacist and racist against White people, particularly the White people who were members of the dominant religion in the area. Dae'quan's views were seen by many as oppositional to the power structure and thus to the institution he worked for.

I was very upset that Dae'quan was losing his job, a loss, incidentally, that would also leave the faculty completely all White. It was at this point that Dae'quan challenged me to do something about it. As the new hire and a recent graduate, I wasn't particularly eager to go in to my new boss and tell him that I felt his decision was incorrect. This was a turning point for me. Was I willing only to commiserate with Dae'quan in private, or would I take a public stand? I felt it was important to me to be loyal to my friend and to match my pronounced beliefs with my actions. I made the appointment and went in to talk to my boss.

Although Dae'quan still lost his job, and my efforts were not even close to what was needed to cause the ruckus necessary in this case to open up the issue of the Whiteness of university faculties, I had made a beginning—puny as it actually was—to speak up against White supremacy. I was determined not be one of those White people who are always trying to hush people of color when they speak out about their experiences of the pain, suffering, and grief that comes from living on the target side of White supremacy—I later would experience this so regularly myself from other White people telling me that I was too radical, too loud, not moderate enough, letting me know that they disapproved of me. I wanted to be strong enough to take the critiques and criticisms from people of color when I kept falling back on White racial knowledge to act in the world. Hence, over time I have worked hard, making many mistakes, some of them big ones, to teach myself and to learn from those around me by positioning myself in contexts and situations that give me opportunities to view the world through the histories, traditions, and wisdoms of people of color rather than with perspectives grounded in the historical privileging of Whiteness.

LITMUS TESTS AND WHITE ALLIES: SOME CONCLUDING THOUGHTS AND HOPES FOR A SOCIALLY JUST FUTURE FOR ALL

It is difficult to write about my journey toward anti-racism all the while knowing that I have not yet arrived, nor am I likely to so-called "fully" arrive in my lifetime—I believe this is why I initially struggled when I received Sara's e-mailed request for answers; I wasn't sure exactly what to say. I also think that everyone's journey will be slightly different depending on their circumstances and the people they find themselves surrounded by.

The difficulty of writing about my journey toward anti-racism lies in the fact that there was no specific huge event that transformed me, nothing like a magical "black box" that I entered as a White person, more-or-less committed to equity, and then exited willing to put all that I have and all that I am on the line for freedom. For me, it has instead been and continues to be more of a day by day process of struggling with the choices I make about whom I interact with, how I conduct myself with them, what books, movies, and other media I consume, what topics I choose to write about, how and where I spend my time and other resources in my personal and professional life.

I make sure, for example, that my circle of friends and acquaintances is not predominantly White and middle-class—I have my students check their *Facebook* pages to consider the Whiteness of their lives, oftentimes much to their chagrin. I likewise chose to move to a predominantly African-American and economically poor neighborhood. My teenagers attended a high school that was over 97% Black.

Yet, here I must offer a strong caution to those sincere Whites who would be allies; I have learned this lesson the hard way both firsthand and from watching other sincere Whites such as White adoptive parents of Black children, and it is a fundamentally important lesson for White people of goodwill (Smith, Jacobson & Juárez, 2012): Just because you live in a Black neighborhood, for example, it does not mean that you are a White person who is an ally in the struggle for social justice. My Malcolm X tattoo tells you nothing about my politics and lifestyle, nor does the fact that my life partner is a Black man. Neither I nor other Whites can point to these associations with people of color, no matter how intimate they are, as markers that I am or you are a "true" White ally in the struggle for social justice.

Just like any other White person, I can live in a Black neighborhood and even be in a long-term domestic relationship, deeply in love with a person of color, and still look at the world around me through the lenses of White racial knowledge: seeing my partner, for example, as the exception to inferiority among Black folk in general and thereby hanging on to my racial group's assumptions of the moral and cultural inferiority of people of color. Moreover, I can also be a White person who lives in an economically poor Black neighborhood and feel that I am some kind of saintly White wonder of a human being coming in here and doing something really exceptional by allowing my Black neighbors to enjoy my company, as truly patronizing as that soundss. In short, I can physically position and symbolically align myself with people of color and still be premising my life and interpreting the world around me in ways that fundamentally continue to reinforce White supremacy and its historical privileging of Whiteness thereby sustaining myself as superior to the people of color around me.

It personally took me a long time to figure out that the notion that all these White women with Black men are automatically very radical or allies in social justice is a completely false assumption with no empirical evidence to support it. Indeed, there is much evidence to the contrary. White women romantically linked with Black men, moreover, is a historical pattern deeply mired in systemic racism, sexism, and classism—as the number of Black men lynched over White women attests (hooks, 1989).

Until a sincere White person is able to view the immediate situation as an instance in the present that is part of these historical patterns that support White supremacy, it is unlikely that any type of work toward social justice will be had from them; this is a critical analytical skill that must and can be acquired by White people, the evidence of which is everywhere around us. Again with Baldwin (1985)—*it might was well be written in the sky.*

Finally, I do not know at this point what has happened to Sara in her journey toward anti-racism. I do not know if I was able to shed any light on the process for her. Nor do I know if she is still in the fight or has settled for the easier road of comfort and security within the liberal bounds of crying out for equality and social justice while acting in ways that ensure that any endeavors toward that end are derailed. Over the years, I have seen many of my students ask the same questions that Sara asked and get very excited about trying to meet the challenges of anti-racism only to face their first challenges and sink back into the safety of Whiteness.

More hopefully, I have also seen many of my students go on to keep learning and struggling toward anti-racism, not turning their face from the hardships that anti-racism will require of them. I am encouraged by these students who continue learning despite the magnitude of the task. I am hopeful because these students will be teachers, and they are part of the next generation of freedom fighters. I hope that some of my story will also help others who seek to push forward in the struggle toward social justice and against Whiteness and White supremacy. I hope that Sara is now learning to help prepare the next generation of freedom fighters in our nation's public schools who are willing to take the bullet for social justice and freedom for all.

B. JUÁREZ

NOTE

¹   Official Third Year Departmental Review letter, Spring, 2010.

REFERENCES

Aptheker, H. (1993). *Anti-racism in U.S. history: The first two hundred years.* Westport, CT: Praeger.
Baldwin, J. (1962/1993). *The fire next time.* New York: Vintage Books.
Baldwin, J. (1985). *The price of a ticket: Collected non-fiction 1948–1985.* New York: St. Martin's Press.
Bennett, L. Jr. (1964). Tea and sympathy: Liberals and other white hopes. In Bennett, L. Jr., (Ed) *The Negro mood and other essays.* (pp. 75–104). Chicago: Johnson Publishing Company.
Bennett, L. Jr. (1972). *The challenge of blackness.* Chicago: Johnson Publishing Company, Inc.
Breitman, G. (Ed.) (1965). *Malcolm X speaks.* New York: Grove Press.
Bonilla-Silva, E. (2003). *Racism without racists: Colorblind racism and the persistence of racial inequality in the United States.* Boulder: Rowman & Littlefield Publishers, Inc.
Cone, J. (2004). *Martin & Malcolm & America: A dream or a nightmare.* Maryknoll, NY: Orbis Books.
Douglass, F. (1845/2001). *Narrative of the life of Frederick Douglass: An American slave written by himself.* New Haven, CT: Yale University Press.
DuBois, W. E. B. (1935). Does the Negro need separate schools? *Journal of Negro Education, 4*(3), 328–335.
DuBois, W. E. B. (1973). *The Education of black people: Ten critiques,* 1906–1960 edited by Herbert Aptheker, Monthly Review Press.
Feagin, J. (2009). *The white racial frame: Centuries of racial framing and counter-framing.* New York: Routledge.
Frankenberg, R. (1997). *Displacing Whiteness.* Durham, NC: Duke University Press.
Gillborn, D. (2005). Education policy as an act of white supremacy: Whiteness, critical race theory and education reform. *Journal of Education Policy, 20*(4), 485–505.
Harris, V. J. (1992). African American conceptions of literacy: A historical perspective. *Theory into Practice, 34*(4), 276–286.
Harris, C. (1995). Whiteness as property. In K. Crenshaw, N. Gotanda, G. Peller, & K. Thomas (Eds.). *Critical race theory: The key writings that formed the movement* (pp. 276–291). New York: The New Press.
Hayes, C., & Juárez, B. G. (2012). There is no culturally responsive teaching here: A critical race theory Perspective. *Democracy and Education, 20*(1), 1–14. http://democracyeducationjournal.org/home/vol20/iss1/1
Hayes, C., & Juárez, B. G. (2009). You showed your Whiteness: You don't get a "good" white peoples medal. *International Journal of Qualitative Studies in Education, 22*(6), 729–744.
hooks, b. (1989). *Talking back: thinking feminist, thinking black.* Boston, MA: South End Press.
Juárez, B. G., Smith, D. T., & Hayes, C. (2008). Social justice means just us white people. *Democracy & Education, 17*(3), 20–25.
Juárez, B. G., & Hayes, C. (2010). Social justice is not spoken here: Considering the nexus of knowledge, power, and the education of future teachers in the United States. *Power and Education, 2*(3), 233–252.
Juárez, B. G., & Hayes, C. (2012). An endarkened learning and transformative education for Freedom Dreams: The Education Our Children Deserve. *The Journal of Educational Controversy, 6*(1), 1–17. http://www.wce.wwu.edu/Resources/CEP/eJournal/v006n001/a007.shtml.
Killens, J. O. (1965). *Black man's burden.* New York: Pocket Books.
King, M. L. Jr. (1964). *Letter from Birmingham jail.* In A. F. Westin, (Ed.) *Freedom Now! The civil rights struggle in America.* (pp. 10–21). New York: Basic Books.
King, R. H. (1996). *Civil rights and the idea of freedom.* Athens: The University of Georgia Press.
Leonardo, Z. (2005). *Race, Whiteness, and education.* New York: Routledge.
Lester, J. (1968). *Look out, Whitey! Black power's gon' get your mama!* New York: Grove Press, Inc.
Mills, C. W. (1997). *The racial contract.* Ithaca: Cornell University Press.
Painter, N. I. (2010). *The history of White people.* New York: W. W. Norton & Company.

Picca, L. H., & Feagin, J. R. (2007). *Two-faced racism: Whites in the backstage and frontstage*. New York: Routledge.

Quarles, B. (1974). *Allies for freedom and blacks on John Brown*. New York: Da Capo Press.

Smith, D., Jacobson, C., & Juárez, B. G. (2012). *White parents, black children: Understanding adoption and race*. New York: Rowman and Littlefield.

Sue, D. W., Capodilupo, C. M., Torino, G. C., Bucceri, J. M., Holder, A. M. B., Nadal, K. L., & Esquilin, M. (2007). Racial micro-aggressions in everyday life: Implications for clinical practice. *American Psychologist, 62*(4), 271–286.

Thurston, B. (2012). *How to be black*. New York: HarperCollins.

Ture, K., & Hamilton, C. V. (1967). *Black power: The politics of liberation in America*. New York: Vintage Books.

Washington, H. A. (2006). *Medical apartheid: The dark history of medical experimentation on black Americans from colonial times to the present*. New York: Broadway Books.

West, C. (1993). *Prophetic thought in postmodern times*. Monroe, ME: Common Courage Press.

West, C. (1997). I'm ofay, you're ofay: A conversation with Noel Ignatiev and William "Upski" Wimsatt. *Transition, 73*, 176–203.

Woodson, C. G. (1933/2000). *The mis-education of the Negro*. Chicago: African American Images.

Wright, R. (1957). *White man listen!* Garden City, NY: Anchor Books.

KARLA MARTIN

4. PRIVILEGING PRIVILEGE WITH THE HOPE OF ACCESSING PRIVILEGE

Dear Academics,

We all use the knowledge that we have learned to make sense of the world around us. I am a young, southern, Poarch Creek woman who has been raised by an amazing family and community. I stand affirmed in my identity and the values of my people. Some of those values are respect, love, and commitment to family and community. I have been taught to think of myself as one part of a larger community, so everything that I do is with the help of others and should be to benefit the larger community.

For the past seven years, I have been in the academy in graduate school and teaching at the university level. I entered this journey with a passion for learning about the field of education, particularly Native American education. In graduate school there were many hoops that I had to jump through and lots of things that caused me to constantly question why I was pursuing an advanced degree. Many times I thought I wasn't smart enough to be in school and wanted to quit. Other times I felt like there was no purpose in putting up with all of the bureaucracy of the academy and felt like I was wasting my time. Getting through my Masters and Doctoral programs was a constant push and pull, but I never quit because of my commitment to my community. I did not enter graduate school thinking about myself, so quitting seemed like a selfish decision to make. Instead I knew that I had come so far and my degree would allow me to be a voice for my tribe and other Indigenous peoples in areas that we do not have access to or have little access to now.

Going into academia after surviving graduate school was a hard decision but one that I eventually made. Many days I wonder if this is the right career choice and question my purpose for being part of this academic institution. I often have to remind myself why I chose to be in the academy in the first place...to give a voice to Indigenous people that are often forgotten, to be an advocate for people of color, and to educate others about Indigenous people.

The longer I stay in academia the clearer I can see a map of academia. I am beginning to understand the ways that academia is entrenched in the privilege and power that upholds a system of Whiteness that automatically benefits some and fails others. Whiteness is often centered as the unspoken standard that everyone else should conform to and will be judged by. Policing of this standard happens every day and gets labeled as "professionalism." What I see happening is that "professionalism" is used as a code word for making Whiteness the standard for

C. Hayes and N.D. Hartlep (Eds.), Unhooking from Whiteness:
The Key to Dismantling Racism in the United States, 53–56.
© *2013 Sense Publishers. All Rights Reserved.*

behavior. Everyone must talk in a certain tone, raise their hand or wait their turn before commenting, be polite, use the appropriate language, and be involved in all department/college gatherings. Politeness, in and of itself, is generally considered a good thing, but it can be misused as a false charge by labeling someone as impolite or rude in order to suppress the content of what the person is trying to communicate. That is the over-arching point I am making here. When people do not fall within the rules of Whiteness they are labeled as rude, inappropriate, or not team players, as if something is wrong with them, not something is wrong with the rules that they are judged by.

What becomes discouraging for me is that there are constant roadblocks I encounter within this system of Whiteness because I do not fit within it. My worldviews and ways of being are very different than those valued in the academy. Actually, in many ways they are opposite of the academy's values. Therefore as I reflect on where I am and have been on this academic map, I find myself hidden, pushed to the margins or deleted.

Almost every day, I see and experience people of color in the academy being surveillanced, silenced, devalued, and disrespected by academics upholding the institution that privileges and operates in Whiteness. For me and other faculty of color who do not buy into this system and choose to answer to our communities first, we fight battles every day resisting the values and ways of the academy. Our commitments are to our communities. They are more difficult judges than the academy will ever be because to them people matter first. At our core we know, value, and live by the rules of our communities and work in ways that are culturally appropriate because that's our standard and the one we choose to be judged by. We name ourselves, do the work that needs to be done, and stay connected to our people. The rules we live by and the goals we strive for oftentimes do not align with academia's way of operating. For us, getting tenure and publishing articles is not our end-all-be-all goal. If an institution is not supportive, we will not stay. If they do not want to hear us talk, we will continue to speak until we decide to speak no more. We would never exploit our communities for academia's goals and the purposes of publishing. In the end we choose our communities and let their voices guide us because if we fail them, we know we have failed.

What makes resisting a daily struggle is that many academics both white and of color have become so invested in these systems. These academics buy into the systems of inequality and begin to judge other's ability and worth by things such as professionalism, tenure, and publications. Their judgments are not based on communities' criteria but on academia's criteria. Therefore, these academics begin to perpetuate a system that harms others with the little power that they have earned. By buying into this system and upholding its values, they then feel protected by the system where in reality they have very little power. In the end, the system will win at the cost of any person, so how much protection does any one person really have?

This reminds me so much about what I have learned about colonization. Colonizers teach the colonized how to colonize one another by using the rules that the colonizers have created. Over time, the colonized are colonizing one another, and the colonizers just sit back and watch with little or no work to do. In the academy this happens almost like clockwork. The rules for things such as tenure, promotion, professionalism, teaching become so engrained that academics begin to judge other academics based on academia's standard for how an academic should look, behave, teach, research, and serve. When academics buy into this system instead of unhooking from it, they see the current benefits but fail to see the long-term consequences for all people.

For me the hardest part of this whole system is working with people who claim to be social justice advocates and who say they push the boundaries and are always raising awareness of injustice. I have met very few scholars who are truly social justice advocates. Such scholars speak up against injustices as they see them happening without skipping a beat. For these few scholars their hearts and commitments are truly focused on social justice, and they live their lives in ways that honor all people and communities. These scholars never stop to think "What's in it for me?" but instead would give up anything they have to stand up for what they believe is right. These scholars are rare and hard to find. However, there are many scholars who claim to be social justice advocates but are so focused on themselves that they don't know how to operate in any kind of selfless way. If it is something that benefits them, then they are all in and want you to be on their side, but when you need help they are either nowhere to be found or are not willing to give up their power and privilege for anyone or any cause. I have seen this play out in many ways. For example, such "fair-weather friend" academics will encourage you to speak up and speak out against the way you have been mistreated, but whenever they see you being mistreated they will not take up for you or help you fight the mistreatment because it has no direct effect on them. Another example is when people of color buy into these systems of Whiteness and say they are radical and social justice people but sit back and say or do nothing. Instead they are used as examples that other people of color are measured by. When people of color don't "measure up" to this standard of Whiteness then it's their fault, not a fault in the system. These are three ways that show how Whiteness works in academic institutions. The last two examples show how Whiteness is masked and, therefore, will continue to exist because only lip service is given to change so that no real change will ever occur.

My question to you is what are you doing to uphold this system of Whiteness that automatically guarantees some success and others failure? How have you bought into this system, and how do you use it to judge students and faculty in this system? For me personally, I have chosen to always be who I am and to stand for what I believe. I have chosen to speak up and out against injustice. What I have found is that when I speak up against injustices that I see, the first comment most academics, almost instinctively make is to blame me for what is happening, and the first question they ask me is what I have done about it. I always find it interesting that others' investment in the academy puts blinders up to the injustices that I am seeing, naming, experiencing, and calling attention to daily. People would rather put a pacifier in my mouth or take me out of a conversation than really listen to what is really happening in the academy and do something about it. Doing something forces people to give up power and privileges that they are too comfortable with and not willing to live without.

There are many people in society who have shared these thoughts before. I write this not because it is something new, but because at this moment in time this is the story that I feel needs to be told. As I hear of people who have positive experiences in academia, I have some hope that there are places within academic institutions that can be supportive for people like me. However, if we continue to use the spaces that we have to speak out, then hopefully our voices will be heard, and maybe these systems or at least spaces within these systems will begin to change.

While all of these things bother others and me, I constantly remind myself that the academy is not where my investment lies. While the personal attacks and negative treatment chip away at my soul, my community rejuvenates me. In the end, my community is where my allegiances lie, and with them is where I find love, peace, comfort, and family...everything that I will ever need. As I think about the future, I have no doubt that I will continue to resist these systems of Whiteness and honor my commitments to my community, for they are the ultimate judge of my character, service, and work.

Sincerely,
Karla Martin, Ph.D.

NICHOLAS D. HARTLEP

5. I REFUSE TO BE A PAWN FOR WHITENESS

A Korean Transracial Adoptee Speaks Out

> In our lack of awareness we can become mere *pawns* of dominance, perpetuating the legitimizing myths that have kept Whites in control for centuries. If we do not understand dominance, we cannot hope to transcend it.
>
> —Howard (1999), p. 47, italics added

This chapter utilizes an autoethnographic methodology (Reed-Danahy, 1997), beginning with the premise that my personal perspective (or *my* standpoint) is uniquely *my* own. I must write that James Baldwin's oft-quoted declaration that "I can't believe what you say, because I see what you do" has been at the forefront of my life, and speaks to the heart of this chapter and of this book: realizing social democracy and fighting racism requires Whites[1] and people of color to unhook from Whiteness (Smith, 2007). For me, unhooking means that I must refuse to be a pawn for Whiteness. Chang (1999) rightly points out, "To the extent that Asian Americans accept the model minority myth, we are complicit in the oppression of other racial minorities and poor Whites" (p. 58).

First, in this chapter I develop the importance that antiracist and critical race theoretical work be done by non-Whites for non-Whites. I label this the FUBU (for us by us) principle. Second, I extend my thoughts on why White co-option is a problem and why Whites (if they truly are freedom fighters) must unhook themselves from their own Whiteness and the Whiteness inured in institutional and social structures in order for social and racial democracy to be realized (Lubiano, 1997). Whiteness, I argue, is largely a Black and White framed issue of social, political, and educational import, simultaneously serving as the context of the present autoethnographic work. Third, I highlight omnipresent questions that I ask myself daily, such as: "Where do I fit as a transracial adoptee in social justice education work?" "Where do yellow-bodied social justice-oriented educators fall in a dualistic continuum from White to Black?" "Am I consciously refusing to be a *pawn* for Whiteness?" The ideas presented in this chapter take on new life when readers view them from a slightly different point of view because, as Wilmot (2005) says, "the very idea that a person can 'give up' Whiteness as an identity is troubling" (p. 84).

C. Hayes and N.D. Hartlep (Eds.), Unhooking from Whiteness:
The Key to Dismantling Racism in the United States, 57–70.
© *2013 Sense Publishers. All Rights Reserved.*

CRITICAL RACE THEORY WITHOUT FOLKS OF COLOR:
TOWARD A FUBU PRINCIPLE[2]

Toffler and Toffler (1999) declare that "[t]he illiterate of the 21st Century will not be those who cannot read and write but those who cannot learn, unlearn, and relearn." Critical race theory (henceforward CRT) should consider the Tofflers' statement, especially the "cannot learn" portion. In 2013 CRT turned twenty-four years old, if not older.[3] Unless CRT aggressively reminds White would-be-users that CRT is the work of people of color for people of color, researchers of all races will continue to mollify this hallmark. Lest we forget, CRT's *sine qua non* is that it is a "standpoint theory" (Chang, 1999, p. 72), implying that "perspective matters" and that the theory was created for disempowered groups to (counter)narrate their histories and current statuses, taking their rightful place in the American nation (Chang, 1999, p. 75). This is what Wilmot (2005) is getting at when she states that to be an effective antiracist ally requires "constantly sorting out when to lead and when to follow in this [social and racial justice] fight" (p. 125).

The Jewish Talmud similarly points out, "We don't see things the way they are; we see things the way we are." White antiracist educators need to recognize and acknowledge that their positions and points of view as privileged people may differ from the perspectives and beliefs held by people of color. Like tall mountains, Whites may see a "problem" only to realize that once atop the acme of the mountain, there are many more peaks (in this case, other systemic problems) that come into view that they were not privy to. These new peaks, metaphorically, could be argued to be "experiential histories" and "racialized lives"—two things that Whites do not necessarily possess, having not experienced them firsthand. Indeed, Myles Horton importantly reminded those at his Highlander Folk School that the oppressed know the answers to their own problems.

Whites are not the only ones who must unhook; people of color also need to unhook from Whiteness. Malcolm X famously wrote, "You don't stick a knife in a man's back nine inches and then pull it out six inches and say you're making progress." He went on to declare, "No matter how much respect, no matter how much recognition, Whites show towards me [as a black man], as far as I am concerned, as long as it is not shown to every one of our people in this country, it doesn't exist for me." Malcolm X's declaration is why, as an Asian American, I refuse to be a pawn for Whiteness.

CRT challenges not only a-historicism, but also a-contextualism (Chang, 1999). History, context, and perspective matter; this is why CRT must endure while retaining its FUBU principle. While I do not want to sound glib, I do believe the antiracist scholarship context to be Whiteness, and Whiteness to be something that all races need to unhook from, because "context defines meaning and meaning shifts with its context" (Chun, 1995, p. 99). As Juárez, Smith, and Hayes (2008) write, "Social Justice Means Just Us White People," which requires people of color to recognize their complicity in being what Delgado (1991) calls good majoritarian "role models."

My controversial ideas—that (1) CRT must remain exclusively "property" of non-Whites, and that (2) doing antiracist work requires practitioners to unhook from Whiteness—raises two paramount questions (among others that CRT practitioners and pedagogues should ask themselves): (1) "For what audiences are CRT critiques and antiracist interpretations intended?" and (2) "Why do White antiracists feel that they can or that they need to use CRT tenets when they don't have the racial standpoint, experience, or perspective to adequately use the theory and its accompanying methodologies?" Whites may, in fact, believe that CRT is their property. A salient example of using CRT ineffectively or incorrectly is found in Epstein's (2006) *A Different View of Urban Schools: Civil Rights, Critical Race Theory, and Unexplored Realities*. Epstein uses "CRT" and "realities" in her book's title, when in reality the book contains no mention of CRT foundational writings!

Property: FUBU

The Merriam-Webster Online Dictionary (2011) defines property in legal terms as "the right to possess and use." CRT fights Whiteness as property (Harris, 1993), but it should extend this fight by fighting for a FUBU principle of the theory's usage, possession, and ownership. CRT belongs to non-Whites—it's their theoretical and existential property—and they are the only ones that should be allowed to use it. I believe that the non-Whites who argue that Whites can use CRT should be scrutinized since this line of thought is an example of their unwillingness to unhook from the establishment's Whiteness (which will be explained later in this chapter).

Fighting White co-option should be a chief concern for CRT and antiracist practitioners and pedagogues because Whites can be "passive" paragons of Whiteness (Warren, 2010). Whites can choose when to fight and when to retreat. They do not have an equal stake in the racial struggle for equity, and they can also decide when and when not to engage. Many White antiracists do not understand this idea (e.g., see Wilmot, 2005). However, as an adopted person of color, I too must unhook from Whiteness, along with any entitlements that Whiteness offers me (i.e. honorary Whiteness status).

Critical Race Theory: Toward a FUBU Principle

Warren's (2010) *Fire in the Heart: How White Activists Embrace Racial Justice* embodies my idea that Whites always have the opportunity to exercise their privilege to be passive in times of struggle. Warren (2010), a White anti-racist educator, writes, "Whites may continue to be passive in the face of racism because it aligns with their structural position in American society" (p. 6). What I am arguing for, then, is a "for us by us" or a "FUBU" (Hoffman, 2006) principle for CRT. Indeed, a CRT in which White researchers are allowed to narrate the oppression and subordination that non-Whites experience is, by definition, flawed. If my fear is legitimate, it means that it is often best for the establishment—that is the academy—to "see" minorities but not to "hear" or "listen" to them.

It has been said that the academy wants "majoritarian role-models," to borrow from the title and thesis of Delgado's (1991) law brief. What I believe Delgado (1991) to be describing is that the minorities who are "good role models" are the same individuals who have not "unhooked" themselves from Whiteness. The White establishment's (ab)use of these few tokenized role models is not for their good, but rather for its own. This "being-seen-but-not-heard" (Hartlep & Ellis, 2013, p. 412) discourse is White co-option made manifest since voice and narration are two of the most important elements of "naming one's reality" (Delgado & Stefancic, 2000) and, by default, CRT (Ladson-Billings & Tate, 1995). I believe that CRT must remember the foundational moorings of CRT. I contend that a FUBU principle is a *lingua franca* that researchers of color can use.

WHAT IS THE BIG PROBLEM?

I believe that the worst thing that can happen to CRT and antiracist work is for it to be co-opted by White researchers (e.g., see Suveges, 2010). The co-option of CRT by Whites is deleterious because CRT grew out of struggles with Critical Legal Studies (CLS). Pain within CLS is what motivated its creation and moved it forward. Non-Whites were not given narrative space and were essentially sidelined during the CLS movement. One reason why White co-option is largely imperceptible or "invisible," for lack of a better word, to many is because White CRT infiltration has become more "mainstream," which weakens the CRT movement and its scholarship. The reason infiltration jeopardizes CRT is precisely the reason that Toni Morrison says, "Definitions belong to the definers, not the defined" (2006, p. 220). Oppressed and disempowered populations and scholars need to be allowed space and opportunity to define *their reality*; they do not need Whites to do it for them. And to be honest, how could even well-intentioned White antiracists do this effectively? As a result, Tierney (2003) discusses how *testimonios* must be written by those being oppressed, not by the oppressors. Sure, Whites may experience various forms of oppression, but do they really need CRT? Why cannot they use critical White studies?

Kailin (2002), a White female antiracist, addresses the racism in the process of academic writing and publishing in her book *Antiracist Education: From Theory to Practice*. In her insightful and provocative book, Kailin (2002) contends that antiracists must question the institutions that reproduce inequality and racism, such as the publishing industry. She argues that this requires that non-White antiracists look to "publishers like Third World Press, Transaction Books, Rethinking Schools, or African American Images Press, to name a few examples of the production or alternative counter-hegemonic knowledge" (p. 56) when trying to get their ideas read, given institutional racism and editorial neglect. Notwithstanding, even Kailin doesn't entirely grasp her recommendations—I would argue that *Rethinking Schools* is also tangentially linked to Whiteness. For instance, look at the magazine's editorial membership and authorship. That being said, I do think *RTS* is a wonderful source of information for social justice-oriented people and practitioners (I should know; I taught and earned my Ph.D. in Milwaukee, Wisconsin).

We must recognize that researchers actively support "the possessive investment in Whiteness" (Lipsitz, 1998) through the monopoly that four publishers have on educational materials. Incredibly, McGraw-Hill, Houghton Mifflin, Harcourt, and Pearson represent seventy percent of the textbook industry (Center for Education Reform, 2001; Hartlep, 2010). Considering their influence on what gets read who gets cited, these four companies deeply impact scholarship and thoughts about race. Consequently, I believe that it is highly problematic when Whites begin to, or continue to, define the work of antiracist education and CRT, as well as the terms and definitions these bodies of scholarship employ. If CRT becomes co-opted, then antiracist scholarship doesn't become a vehicle for radical social and racial change, but rather another tool for the maintenance and strengthening of "the possessive investment in Whiteness" (Lipsitz, 1998).

BLACK, WHITE, AND YELLOW: MY REFUSAL TO BE A PAWN FOR WHITENESS

Daniels and Kitano (1970) inform readers that the Black-White binary is perpetuated by five mechanisms that help maintain Whiteness: prejudice, discrimination, segregation, isolation and exclusion, and genocide. As a transracial adoptee, I do not fit neatly into this dual-categorized paradigm, and I actively choose to unhook myself from Whiteness. Specifically, I refuse to be a pawn for Whiteness—*pawn* representing an unwillingness to problematize and speak out about White privilege.

As a racialized and minoritized man, I feel that it is problematic for Whites to do critical race theoretical scholarship, especially when they do not unhook themselves from their own Whiteness and the institutional and structural Whiteness that privileges them, regardless of whether they are truly freedom fighters. I do not, and I cannot, trust many White antiracists and/or critical race theoreticians until I get to know them intimately because I see what they do. This is the message Baldwin was delivering in his quip, "I can't believe what you say, because I see what you do." It is this unwillingness of a few to unhook from Whiteness that catalyzes my refusal to be a pawn for Whiteness. Some label Asian Americans who have not unhooked from Whiteness "Twinkies" (Yellow on the outside and White on the inside). To me, "unhooking from Whiteness" means that as a transracial adoptee and social justice advocate, ally, and dissident, I consistently question my educational and social upbringing along with the colorblind ways of interpreting society and the schooling processes. It is only when I refuse to be a good majoritarian "role model" or a "pawn" that I become a true AsianCrit or antiracist.

Antiracist Work: An Adopted Korean's Point of View

By and large, the recognized and mainstream anti-racist establishment is White (e.g., see Juárez, Smith, & Hayes, 2008). History is chock-full of well-known White men

61

and women who have done or are currently doing antiracist work. Howard Zinn, Myles Horton, John Dewey, Gary Howard, Thomas Galludet, Tim Wise, Herbert Aptheker, Morris Dees, Paul Gorski,[4] and Peggy McIntosh are but a few examples. Some of these White antiracist pioneers were enlisted by non-White antiracists. I want to be clear that I am arguing that unhooking from Whiteness requires *all individuals* (be they White or non-White) to be aware of their loyalties. Unhooking from Whiteness necessitates breaking away from dual loyalties. What does this mean? What are dual loyalties?

Unhooking From Whiteness: Resisting Dual Loyalties

For Whites, namely, resisting dual loyalties requires them to lose out on power, prestige, and privilege that they have historically received as a function of being socially constructed as White. "Unhooking" or White separatism may require a "social suicide" of sorts; this idea is captured in steps five and nine that Hayes, Juárez, Witt, and I outlined in the introduction outlined in the introduction of this edited volume (step five being that White antiracists have to get over themselves; antiracist work is not about them; and step nine being that Whites need to admit that their interests in helping marginalized people are sometimes self-serving).

If racism is ever fully eradicated, which I do not envision happening any time soon,[5] antiracists of all races would be out of work. Thus, Whites need to understand that while they may appear to "want to help," it is possible that they want to help "just enough" so that they continue to reap the rewards. As academicians, rewards are the ability to continue to write books, give lectures, and be recognized as being a social justice "expert." The rewards that the academy gives its professors, in some ways, control them—although this is not always the rule. The hidden motivation of "slow progress" is captured in neo-liberal commentary that indicates that change is slow, and that incremental gains are to be celebrated, not chided. No one needs antiracist *prima donnas* of any race; thus, how a White person can develop expertise in terms of antiracist knowledge is highly questionable to me. This is what I am attempting to get at: I needed to earn a Ph.D. to talk about stuff I already knew and had experienced (i.e., racism, discrimination, inequity).

Moreover, as a transracial Korean adoptee—who is at times ideologically Whitened and at other times Blackened (Hartlep, 2013; Zhou, 2004)—my life experiences inform me that if I wish to be an antiracist practitioner, a pedagogue, and/or an AsianCrit (Chang, 1999), dual loyalties are not possible or permissible. I cannot maintain ties to a racist world—viz. benefit from Whiteness or "honorary" Whiteness (Tuan, 1998)—and simultaneously be an ally and outspoken antiracist for communities of color. This is what Hayes articulates well in his chapter in this volume.

Dual loyalties are diametrically opposed to one another. Unhooking from Whiteness costs a lot (especially for Whites), but earns equity, equality, and social/racial justice by making racism and Whiteness visible and by persuading others to do the same, especially since Whiteness and White privilege are invisible (Rothenberg, 2008). Clearly, then, it is not in the best interest of White antiracists' careers—when looking at the social and economic costs and benefits—to unhook from their own and/or institutional Whiteness. This is precisely why the thought of "unhooking" is so revolutionary and why the present volume is so paradigmatically groundbreaking. Are Whites and non-Whites willing to unhook?

Warren (2010) states that "whites may have a broader or longer-term interest in joining with people of color, which trumps any short-term advantage to white privilege "(p. 7), to which I disagree. As a White male professor, Warren may believe that Whites have such an interest, but there is no such thing as a short-term advantage (at least from my perspective as a person of color) when speaking about individualized or institutionalized White privilege. For instance, when Warren was denied tenure at Harvard, many students and faculty came to his side, arguing—in solidarity with him and on behalf of him—that there was no reason he should not have received tenure. Warren's constituents' aiding and abetting conferred positive press for him, for Warren was being publicly martyred in the academic square, if you will. But if Warren were to be a true antiracist ally, I would argue, he would have refused this attention, and perhaps would have asked himself and Harvard tougher questions. Not why was he denied tenure, but rather: "Why is there a noticeable absence of tenured professors of color at Harvard?" Derrick Bell, a professor of color, took issue with the lack of professors of color in Harvard's Law School long before Warren's tenure was denied. What of Dr. Bells' actions? Why didn't Warren raise concern about a lack of tenured faculty of color?

Informational Narcissism: Non Satis Scire—To Know is Not Enough

Some White antiracists are "informational narcissists." What I mean by this term is that they write about social justice and talk about it, but they never live it or experience it. These sorts of antiracist scholars are consumers of social and racial justice and are, as a result, containers of it. But these very same activists are not community spokespersons, and they are certainly not *lumpen* proletarians given their own White privileged upbringings. I view these White academics are unwilling to lose out on the academic "goodies." Nowhere is this idea of social and racial justice consumption more apparent than in the scholarship of critical race theory. WhiteCrits, to me, are kleptocrats, as Whites are not epistemologically able to write about something they don't in fact experience on a daily basis (i.e., micro-aggressions, micro-invalidations, micro-insults, racial weathering, etc.). This is one of the basic tenets of phenomenological research; the researcher must have experienced the phenomenon of interest and research (Tierney, 2003). To know about race is not the same as to experience it, or in Latin, *Non Satis Scire*—to know is not enough. To know antiracist education is simply not enough. This is also why one of the tenets of critical race theory is "experiential knowledge" (Hartlep, 2010; Horsford, 2011).

By using the framework and theory of critical race theory, Whites benefit when they publish while other non-White critical race theoreticians and epistemologists perish. Everything that has gone wrong with the competitive academic publishing process is on display when "the possessive investment in Whiteness" (Lipsitz, 1998) is maintained and extended. Coming from a working-class background, I am well aware that many Asian American scholar activists historically came from privileged positions in society (Wong, 1972). These Asian American activists too—like middle class White scholars—must unhook from ideological and institutional Whiteness.

Stepping Aside: CRT and White Alliances

I was upset when I learned that Tim Wise was a featured speaker at the Fourth Annual Critical Race Studies in Education Conference (Theme: "Deconstructing Contemporary Post-Racial Discourses") [access at www.creassoc.org] held in Salt Lake, Utah. Why? I believe CREASSOC hurt CRT by inviting Wise, a White "anti-racist author and activist" (taken from the conference flier), because there is an overabundance of scholars of color who would have made excellent speakers (e.g., see Yosso's [2005] article that introduced "WhiteCrit").

Wise rounded out the invited scholar-speakers who were otherwise all scholars and professors of color: Drs. Gloria Ladson-Billings, Octavio Villalpando, William Smith, and Dolores Delgado Bernal. Let me clarify something so that my thoughts are not mollified or misunderstood by readers: at CRT events Wise *can* and *should be* allowed to be a White ally; however, as crass or parochial as it sounds, I feel that White allies must *support*, rather than *give* speeches. Wise, offering his support rather than speaking at CREASSOC, would have better illustrated his willingness to unhook from his own Whiteness. Unhooking from his Whiteness doesn't prevent Wise, a White anti-racist educator, from doing his important antiracist work, but it does require him to relieve himself from taking center stage because CRT should have a FUBU principle as I have argued earlier. Non-Whites don't need White teachers and preachers; they desire authentic allies and advocates.

Personal Experiences: Privileged White Antiracists

A friend of color recently told me that he added Wise as a friend on Facebook. Once accepted as a friend by Wise, my friend posted a question on Wise's Facebook wall: how could he do anti-racist work as a White man, and questioned his motivations? Wise responded by terminating his Facebook friendship, and blocked my friend from viewing or posting on his Facebook wall. By filtering/censoring his wall, Wise put up an artificial barrier to open discourse. Why didn't Wise engage in a publically accessible conversation on his Facebook page? Why was he alarmed that a person of color asked him what motivated him to do anti-racist writing and advocacy work? I speculate the answer is because Wise was unwilling to hear a non-White question his authenticity and credentials for doing the work that he putatively does. While most anti-racist researchers and "experts" undergo rigorous educational training, Wise has been allowed to publish book after book, and continues to be invited to many speaking engagements despite his lack of a formal terminal degree (author's note: he holds only a bachelor's degree, unlike many scholars of color who hold Ph.D.'s and sometimes even have postdoctoral training).[6]

Does Wise support in ways that might lead to personal or professional loss? Other White allies have in times past. Take, for instance, John Brown, a well-known radical American slave abolitionist who had skin in: he was hung for his antiracism agitations and involvement in treasonous activities. I *do* believe that there are authentic White antiracists and allies—the more difficult thing is locating them. Historically, John Brown clearly was one. Contemporarily, Gorski (2012) is one too: he has written some great autoethnographic work detailing this exact predicament: how does he remain authentic and a reputable ally in antiracist education as a privileged person? In the section that follows I discuss authentic alliances.

Authentic Alliances: The Importance of Unhooking from Whiteness

His unwillingness to unhook from Whiteness is why I believe Wise is not a true ally of CRT or communities of color. I am not stating that Wise has ulterior motives; *indeed he has helped* minorities and their communities, and was invited to review chapters for this volume. However, I believe Wise does not have an equally vested interest in realizing racial equity or social justice like people of color do. I believe that there are two reasons why Wise is problematic to CRT and antiracist work when he does not step back from the podium and when he does not unhook from his Whiteness: First, his words do not have the racial or experiential legitimacy that a minority's words have, and second, he is taking away valuable attention from minority scholars who are doing the same work. My concerns are not unfounded, and have been raised by others in decades past. For instance, the Student Nonviolent Coordinating Committee (commonly referred to as SNCC) and Stanley Carmichael as well as advocates of Black Power all worried about being co-opted by the White Peace Movement.

Another reason White co-option is something CRT must fight against is because not only is it a form of "White interest convergence" (Bell, 1980), it also serves as a *status quo* mechanism that the White establishment uses in order to closely monitor research and control radical ideas. bell hooks discusses this in meticulous detail in her essay *Teaching Resistance: The Racial Politics of Mass Media,* found in her book *Killing Rage: Ending Racism* (1995, pp. 108–118). She talks about how "[s]egregation enabled black folks to maintain oppositional worldviews and standpoints to counter the effects of racism and to nurture resistance" (p. 109), and goes on to suggest that "[t]he resistance to colonialism was so fierce, a new strategy was required to maintain and perpetuate White supremacy. Racial integration was that strategy" (p. 109). hooks is onto something: she is not only talking about neocolonial White supremacy; she is speaking toward the idea of White co-option of various movements. Whites have historically appeared to "have cared," only to stay close enough to co-opt or control minority movements of racial and/or political struggle. Wise can unhook if he can agree that there is privilege that he has not yet dealt with, and if he has the humility to seriously consider this evaluation.

Co-opted movements have been swallowed up by organizations and institutions so that they can be closely monitored and controlled by the dominant class. This is why CRT must use a FUBU principle and why a "standpoint theory" requires the narration of non-Whites. hooks' comments support the ideas that Daniels and Kitano (1970) introduced toward the beginning of this chapter: Whiteness adopted integration as a strategy to consolidate its power previously maintained through prejudice, discrimination, segregation, isolation, and exclusion.[7]

Readers of this book generally, and this chapter specifically, need to be reminded that CRT began due to the fact that non-Whites were neither listened to nor taken seriously in the CLS movement. "Their" (read: minorities') voices were marginalized, often muted, and went unheard and unacknowledged within the CLS movement. This being said, I believe that antiracist maven Tim Wise would benefit from listening to scholars who are non-White and who have studied and prepared for a lives and careers as researchers.

CRT IS A STANDPOINT THEORY: WHY THIS MATTERS

For a paper I presented at the Northeastern Educational Research Association (NERA) Annual Meeting (e.g., see Hartlep & Ellis, 2010), my co-author, Antonio Ellis and I analyzed a National dataset taken from the U.S. Department of Education. We found that non-White parents had a higher probability of being involved in their child's homework than Whites. The audience was stunned (dumbfounded would be a better word), and there was pushback against our study's findings. "Are you positive about your findings?" they asked us. Every possible question was thrown our way. The reason that the mainly White audience scrutinized our study's findings was because our paper went against everything the audience believed in. The White crowd of tenured academics and Graduate Students had a difficult time digesting our presentation's findings.

When Antonio and I were tired of fielding their questions, I asked the audience a provocative question of my own. I asked them why they were unable to concede that Black parents were more likely to be involved in their child's homework. I reminded them that they—the audience—were entirely White (100 percent). Specifically, I asked them how they could understand our findings, especially if it went against their own experientially-informed thoughts, paradigms, understandings, and epistemologies of non-White learners. In my mind I knew that many in the audience were "aversive racists" (Gaertner & Dovidio, 1986).

My co-presenter and I were the only minority males in the conference room. I mentioned to the exclusively female audience that it is problematic when more than 80% of our nation's K-12 teachers are White women, and there is a lack of Black and

Asian American male elementary school teachers (Epstein, 2005; King, 1993; Rong & Preissle, 1997; Teranishi, 2010; Toldson, 2011). I urged the conferees to consider that an unbalanced teaching force—in terms of race or gender—leads to unbalanced education for children (Kailin, 2002). I did not remind them that only 1.5% of our nation's K-12 teachers are Asian Americans, but I should have (Teranishi, 2010). These last two statistics further illustrate the importance of race, gender, and culture in education and in antiracist and CRT work (Howard, 2010).

Despite CRT's belief about and need of White alliances (let me be clear, I *do* believe CRT and antiracist work needs White allies), I contend that it still must utilize a FUBU principle and that all antiracist practitioners and pedagogues must unhook themselves from Whiteness. Scholars of color should acknowledge that historically there have been White allies who *have* helped minorities in numerous ways. For instance, Thomas Galludet (the Galludet University was named for him) sitting on the original Board of Trustees for Howard University, and John Dewey helping to form the NAACP (Hansen, 2007). It is clear that these institutions of learning and organizations may not have enjoyed the success they achieved without these White allies. Moreover, let us not forget that there were numerous Quakers during the time of legalized chattel slavery who helped Harriet Tubman and others on the Underground Railroad.

Silent Partners: An Ideal Type of Ally

Clearly, minorities do need White allies to use their White privilege to help in the fight since it is the "other side of racism" (Rothenberg, 2008). However, some White allies have been more instructive and authentic than others. I contend that the ideal type of a White ally is what Takaki (1990, pp. 307–308) calls "silent partners." Takaki was referring to White bankers, lawyers, or farmers who helped the Japanese circumvent the Alien Land Laws in the U.S. during a time when Asians were looked down upon. Thus, "silent partners" were White investors who did not have any management responsibilities but provided capital, resources, and also shared liability for any losses experienced. The silent partners were not practicing "White interest convergence" (Bell, 1980) since they could lose, and many times they did. During the process, these silent partners unhooked from Whiteness too. What do Wise and other White allies lose if CRT and antiracist practitioners lose the battle against White supremacy? Nothing; they don't. Martin outlines this well in her chapter "Privileging Privilege with the Hope of Accessing Privilege": the idea that there is tremendous risk of losing when an individual unhooks from Whiteness.

Frederick Douglass was acutely aware that "we struggle to learn, so we can learn to struggle." I ask readers two questions, "Have we learned from what happened with Critical Legal Studies?" and "Are we are learning to use CRT and antiracist scholarship to advance our causes (toward a FUBU conceptualization of CRT and antiracist work)?" I maintain that CRT is foolish at best, and stupid at worst, not to learn from the history of CLS. If it does not learn, as the Tofflers' (1999) have stressed,

CRT will be doomed to repeat it. Enough is enough; CRT lies in the bed it makes: It is high time that CRT wakes up and does something about the problems raised in this chapter. What can and should CRT and antiracist education do? The first step needs to be to unhook from Whiteness. Unhooking one's self from Whiteness is not an easy task, especially if it means you lose privilege. Chan and Wang (1991) write the following: "But who gets accepted into the inner circles is very selective: Those who won't rock the boat are the most likely to be allowed entry. The presence of such individuals is not threatening because they will help to perpetuate the system, and not change or destroy it" (pp. 59–60). Reverend William Sloane Coffin once said, "If you stand for nothing you will fall for anything." Malcolm X echoed that sentiment: "A man who stands for nothing will fall for anything."

I do not fall for the "goodies" Whiteness privileges me with as a model minority: honorary Whiteness. I refuse to be a pawn for Whiteness because that is what I must do to be a freedom fighter. According to Cho (1994), "When we [Asian Americans] refuse to play the role of the loyal Uncle Tom or the upstanding Model Minority, we also deny [society] a valuable mouthpiece to be used to front for and exonerate a racist United States" (p. 271). Similarly, Cho (1994) notes that "Clarence Thomas personifies for black communities in this country what the *model minority myth* and its legacy does to working Asians" (p. 257, italics added). Malcolm X famously asked, "What do you call a Black man with a PhD?" He responded to his own question, "A nigger."

Whiteness wants me to be its pawn so that it can divide-and-conquer people of color. My choice is resistance through rejection and refutation of the passive, quiet, and sullen Asian American. As Howard (1999) noted in this chapter's epigraph, "In our lack of awareness we can become mere pawns of dominance, perpetuating the legitimizing myths that have kept Whites in control for centuries. If we do not understand dominance, we cannot hope to transcend it."

NOTES

[1] I choose to capitalize racial categories in my chapter to emphasize their social and cultural significance. Black and African American are used interchangeably.

[2] I have drawn this title from Dr. Thandeka K. Chapman (Associate Professor at the University of Wisconsin-Milwaukee). Chapman's idea appears in a paper that we (a team of 5) presented at the 2011 AERA Annual Meeting held in New Orleans, LA, titled "FUBU (ForUsByUs) Style: Researchers of Color Documenting the Lives of Students of Color in Majority White Suburban Schools."

[3] It has been written that in either 1977 or 1989 CRT made its debut at a workshop held at St. Benedict Center in Madison, Wisconsin (see Taylor, Gillborn, & Ladson-Billings, 2009; see also Delgado & Stefancic, 2001).

[4] Gorski (2012) has written an excellent critique of Peggy McIntosh's work in his essay "Complicating White Privilege: Poverty, Class, and the Nature of the Knapsack" published in *Teachers College Record*.

[5] CRT argues that racism is a normal and not an aberrational phenomenon. Racism is not going away without a fight.

[6] This does not mean that I fully support formal education, *per se*, since in many ways education is riven with Whiteness and processes that maintain unequal educative and political realities.

[7] For example, read Dudziak's (1998) article, "Desegregation as a Cold War Imperative"

REFERENCES

Bell, D. (1980). *Brown v. Board of Education* and the interest convergence dilemma. *Harvard Law Review, 93*(3), 518–533.

Center for Education Reform. (2001, May). *The textbook conundrum.* Retrieved on May 11, 2012 from http://edreform.com/_upload/textbook.pdf

Chan, S., & Wang, L. (1991). Racism and the model minority: Asian-Americans in higher education. In P. G. Altbach & K. Lomotey (Eds.) *The racial crisis in American higher education* (pp. 43–67). New York, NY: State University of New York Press.

Chang, R. S. (1999). *Disoriented: Asian Americans, law, and the nation-state.* New York, NY: New York University Press.

Cho, M. (1994). Overcoming our Legacy as cheap labor, scabs, and model minorities. In K. Aguilar-San Juan (Ed.) *The state of Asian America: Activism and resistance in the 1990s* (pp. 253–273). Boston, MA: South End Press.

Chou, R. S., & Feagin, J. R. (2008). *The myth of the model minority: Asian Americans facing racism.* Boulder, CO: Paradigm Publishers.

Chun, K. (1995). The myth of Asian American success and its educational ramifications. In D. T. Nakanishi & T. Y. Nishida (Eds.) *The Asian American educational experience.* New York, NY: Routledge.

Daniels, R., Kitano, H. (1970). *American racism: Exploration of the nature of prejudice.* Englewood Cliffs, NJ: Prentice-Hall.

Delgado, R. (1991). Affirmative action as a majoritarian device: Or, do you really want to be a role model? *Michigan Law Review, 89*(5), 1222–1231.

Delgado, R., & Stefancic, J. (2001). *Critical Race Theory: An Introduction.* New York, NY: New York University Press.

Dudziak, M. L. (1988). Desegregation as a cold war imperative. *Stanford Law Review, 41*(1), 61–120.

Epstein, K. K. (2006). *A Different view of urban schools: Civil rights, critical race theory, and unexplored realities.* New York, NY: Peter Lang.

Epstein, K. K. (2005). The whitening of the American teaching force: A problem of recruitment or a problem of racism? *Social Justice, 32*(3), 89–102.

Gaertner, S. L., & Dovidio, J. F. (1986). The aversive form of racism. In J. F. Dovidio & S. L. Gaertner (Eds.) *Prejudice, discrimination and racism: Theory and research* (pp. 61–89). Orlando, FL: Academic Press.

Gorski, P. C. (2012). Complicating white privilege: Poverty, class, and the nature of the knapsack. *Teachers College Record.* Accessed April 3, 2012, from http://www.tcrecord.org/Content.asp?ContentID=16687

Hansen, D. T. (2007). *Ethical visions of education: Philosophies in practice.* New York, NY: Teachers College Press.

Harris, C. I. (1993). Whiteness as property. *Harvard Law Review, 106*(8), 1707–1791.

Hartlep, N. D. (2010). *Going public: Critical race theory and issues of social justice.* Mustang, OK: Tate Publishing.

Hartlep, N. D. (2013). White privilege: Do transracial Korean adoptees have it? *Korean Quarterly, 16*(2), 22.

Hartlep, N. D., & Ellis, A. L. (2010). Are household income, gender, and race important in shaping parental involvement in children's education? *NERA Conference Proceedings.* Retrieved on April 3, 2012 from http://digitalcommons.uconn.edu/cgi/viewcontent.cgi?article=1006&context=nera_

Hartlep, N. D., & Ellis, A. L. (2013). Rethinking speech and language impairments within fluency dominated cultures. In S. Pinder (Ed.) *American multicultural studies* (pp. 411–429). Thousand Oaks, CA: Sage Publications.

Horsford, S. D. (2011). *Learning in a burning house: Educational inequality, ideology, and (dis)integration.* New York, NY: Teachers College Press.

Howard, G. R. (1999). *We can't teach what we don't know: White teachers, multiracial schools.* New York, NY: Teachers College Press.

Howard, T. C. (2010). *Why race and culture matter in schools: Closing the achievement gap in America's classrooms.* New York, NY: Teachers College Press.

Juárez, B. G., Smith, D. T., & Hayes, C. (2008). Social justice means just us white people: The diversity paradox in teacher education. *Democracy & Education, 17*(3), 20–25.

Kailin, J. (2002). *Antiracist education: From theory to practice.* Lanham, MD: Rowman & Littlefield.

King, J. H. (1993). The limited presence of African-American teachers. *Review of Educational Research, 63*(2), 115–149.

Ladson-Billings, G., & Tate, W. F. (1995). Toward a critical race theory of education. *Teachers College Record, 97*(1), 47–68.

Lipsitz, G. (1998). *The possessive investment in Whiteness: How white people profit from identity politics.* Philadelphia, PA: Temple University Press.

Lubiano, W. (Ed). (1997). *The house that race built.* New York, NY: Vintage books.

Matsuda, M. (1993, February). Voices of the community: We will not be used. *Asian American & Pacific Islands Law Journal, 1,* 79–84.

Merriam-Webster Online Dictionary (2011). *Entry for property.* Retrieved May 17, 2011 from http://www.m-w.com/dictionary/property

Reed-Danahy, D. E. (1997). *Auto/ethnography: Rewriting the self and the social.* New York, NY: Oxford University Press.

Rong, X. L., & Preissle, J. (1997). The continuing decline in Asian American teachers. *American Educational Research Journal, 34*(2), 267–293.

Rothenberg, P. S. (Ed.) (2008). *White privilege* (3rd ed.). New York, NY: Worth Publishers.

Smith, C. (2007). *The cost of privilege: Taking on the system of white supremacy and racism.* Fayetteville, NC: Camino Press.

Stalvey, L. M. (1989). *The education of a WASP.* Madison, WI: University of Wisconsin Press.

Taylor, E., Gillborn, D, and Ladson-Billings (Eds). (2009). *Foundations of critical race theory in education.* New York: Routledge.

Teranishi, R. T. (2010). *Asians in the ivory tower: Dilemmas of racial inequality in American higher education.* New York, NY: Teachers College Press.

Tierney, W. G. (2003). Undaunted courage: Life history and the postmodern challenge. In N. K. Denzin & Y. S. Lincoln (Eds.), *Strategies of qualitative inquiry* (pp. 292–318). Thousand Oaks, CA: Sage Publications.

Toffler, A., & Toffler, H. (1999). Foreword. In: Gibson, R. (Ed.). *Rethinking the future: Rethinking Business principles, competition, control and complexity, leadership, markets and the world.* London: Nicholas Brealey Publishing.

Toldson, I. (2011). Diversifying the United States' teaching force: Where are we now? Where do we need to go? How do we get there? *The Journal of Negro Education, 80*(3), 183–186.

Tuan, M. (1998). *Forever foreigners or honorary whites? The Asian ethnic experience today.* New Brunswick, NJ: Rutgers University Press.

Warren, M. R. (2010). *Fire in the heart: How White activists embrace racial justice.* New York, NY: Oxford University Press.

Wilmot, S. (2005). *Taking responsibility taking direction: White anti-racism in Canada.* Winnipeg, Manitoba, Canada: Arbeiter Ring Publishing.

Wise, T. (2008). *White like me: Reflections on race from a privileged son.*

Wong, P. (1972). The emergence of the Asian-Americans movement. *Bridge, 2*(1), 32–39.

Zhou, M. (2004). Are Asian Americans becoming "white?" *Contexts, 3*(1), 29–37.

KENNETH J. FASCHING-VARNER, MARGARET-MARY SULENTIC
DOWELL, DANA L. BICKMORE & STEVEN BICKMORE

6. REPOSITIONING THE HOOK

(Re)committing to Equity Through Autoethnographic Exploration

INTRODUCTION

The framing of this volume has centered on the notion of unhooking from Whiteness as a mechanism to dismantle racism. For many scholars of color, being hooked by Whiteness has represented not only a well-researched problematic of race (Fasching-Varner, 2009), but being hooked by Whiteness has assigned a particular property value to Whiteness and Blackness determined by the White majority (Harris, 1995; Ladson-Billings & Tate, 1995; Dixson & Rousseau, 2006; Fasching-Varner, 2009). For White scholars, though, the act of unhooking from Whiteness, in an ironic way, relieves the White academic from the responsibility of Whiteness. As authors of this chapter we range in age, gender, religious background, socioeconomic status, and childhood socialization experiences, yet we all share the mantle of Whiteness and the ensuing racism of Whiteness – we are in fact on the hook for Whiteness, and necessarily so. We struggle with unhooking ourselves from Whiteness, or perhaps we should posit that we may even be incapable of doing so, despite how tempting such a move may be. However, we recognize that for scholars of color, the act of unhooking from Whiteness is necessary.

The editors who issued the call for chapters for this volume suggested that unhooking from Whiteness "…requires courage, boldness, and much risk-taking." We are skeptical, in the way racial-realist Bell (1995) is skeptical, of a perspective that would frame us as being unhooked from Whiteness; such an unhooking would necessarily imply that we have moved beyond race, that we *could* move beyond race. Our commitment to enacting perspectives centered in boldness and risk taking requires not that we unhook, but rather look at how we, as White educators, will always be on the hook by and for Whiteness, and to confront our Whiteness and ourselves. If Whiteness, and the racism derived from Whiteness, has been the major operating perspective within the United States (U.S.) landscape, then careful attention should be paid to understanding the everyday ways in which racism and Whiteness operate, particularly within the academy. Our position, then, requires that we explore the implications of our Whiteness, in essence repositioning the hook so that the connection to Whiteness becomes a productive mechanism to work against racism, though we are inherently racist anti-racists (Clark & O'Donnell, 1999).

C. Hayes and N.D. Hartlep (Eds.), Unhooking from Whiteness:
The Key to Dismantling Racism in the United States, 71–91.
© *2013 Sense Publishers. All Rights Reserved.*

We organized the chapter as follows: First, we briefly explore related literature to help contextualize this work. Second, we provide a methodological overview of how we used autoethnography to frame our work, particularly focusing on our process of revealing narratives that exemplify how Whiteness has hooked us in our own professional/personal lives. From that departure point, we each share narratives of our own Whiteness, in author order, that we believe show why we will necessarily always be on the hook when it comes to Whiteness. To be clear, these narratives are not coming-out stories where we reveal a consciousness of racism to be left at the level of coming to know – such a perspective would reify and center Whiteness. Our narratives are deployed to show that across the intersections of our identities, which range in age, class, and socio-economic status, Whiteness is ever present in our lives. Due to its presence, we have an obligation to be vocal about how it operates, especially with Whiteness' potential to reify hegemony. Finally, we share some implications that our autoethnographic narratives reveal that may be helpful for other educators.

THE LITERATURE

As chapter authors, we situate our work within the base of understanding that there is a pervasive investment in Whiteness and the property value of Whiteness that has shaped historical and contemporary racism in the U.S. As such, we wish to briefly explore some extant literature from Critical Race Theory (CRT) and Whiteness to provide a theoretical frame and context for how we come to present our narratives later in the chapter.

Critical Race Theory

Educational scholars and researchers have used CRT to analyze the ways in which race impacts educational outcomes (Hartlep, 2010; Ladson-Billings & Tate, 1995; Tate, 1994; Taylor, 2000; Delgado Bernal & Villapando, 2002; Duncan, 2002; Dixson & Rousseau, 2005; DeCuir & Dixson, 2004; Tate & Rousseau, 2002; Solorzano & Yosso, 2002; Fasching-Varner, 2009; 2013). Whiteness as property (Harris, 1995; Ladson-Billings, 1999; Dixson & Rousseau, 2006; Fasching-Varner, 2009; Fasching-Varner, 2013), a particular concept used within CRT work, serves as a theoretical lens by which the narratives of many White educators can be understood. Harris (1995) outlines the conditions by which society constructs Whiteness as property, implying that there is an absoluteness or inalienability to Whiteness, which allows for people vested in Whiteness to experience a high sense of value for said Whiteness. Often falsely understood at the level of phenotype (Hall, 1997; Montague, 1997; Winant, 2000), to possess Whiteness is an absolute that garners a higher value as property.

Harris (1995) cites that White peoples capitalize on their Whiteness for purposes of enjoyment, placing high value on the reputation of Whiteness. For example, calling a White person "*Black,*" can cause potential harm to his/her reputation, devaluing one's Whiteness. Whiteness excludes since White people never have to, and rarely do, define Whiteness. The more common approach is defining what Whiteness is not, and in so doing White people exclude all those deemed to not possess Whiteness. The nature of how Whiteness is not defined, in tandem with the absolute nature of Whiteness, provides a space whereby Whiteness serves a property function—unhooking from the unpleasant aspects of Whiteness, namely racism—and creates a space to buttress the value of Whiteness while absolving oneself of personal responsibility for racism. Critical Race Theory scholars (Harris, 1995; Morrison, 1993; Crenshaw, 1995; Ladson-Billings & Tate, 1996; Tate & Rousseau, 2002; Dixson & Rousseau, 2006; Fasching-Varner, 2009; Fasching & Mitchell, 2013) all discuss, to some extent, the role of expansive vs. restrictive constructions of race. The expansive view of anti-discrimination policies conceives of ending the conditions and circumstances by which the subordination of Black peoples exist, working "to further the national goal for eradicating the effects of racial oppression" (Crenshaw, 1995, p. 105). On the other hand, restrictionists posit that discriminatory acts take place in isolation, are targeted at individuals, and are not representative of policies targeted to whole groups (Dixson & Rousseau, 2004; Crenshaw, 1995). To this extent, restrictionists are sheltered from dealing with race outside very narrowly constructed, localized, and historical experiences and contexts, and thus are able to lodge racial critiques. The act of White people attempting to unhook from Whiteness is seemingly expansive; however, the effect for White people is a reification of the very racism that is a part of being on the hook for Whiteness. That is, without naming the way in which White people are always hooked by Whiteness, White-racism can be disguised by expansive-sounding discourse despite restrictive behaviors around race and racism.

Whiteness

Whiteness has become a popular lens of study over the past 20 years (Ignatiev, 1995, 1997a, 1997b; Lipsitz, 1998, 2005, 2006; Hartigan, 1999; López, 2006; Roediger, 1991, 1994, 1997, 1998, 2004; Smedley, 1998; Carter, Helms, & Juby, 2004; Applebaum, 2007; Reason, 2007; Philipsen, 2003; Giroux, 1997, and Hurtado, 1999). In this cited literature, a pervasive theme is a commitment to examining Whiteness in the context of continually changing cultural environments. Hurtado (1999) suggests that "we have yet to chronicle how those who oppress make sense of their power in relationship to those they have injured" (p. 226). By exploring Whiteness from a variety of perspectives, theories of Whiteness are thought to be exploring the "powerful means of critiquing the reproduction and maintenance of systems of racial inequality"—whether or not such critique has been met is up for debate (Hartigan, 1999, p. 183). Similarly, Lipsitz (2005 and 2006) warns not to ignore "the possessive investment in Whiteness and invert the history of racial politics in the United States" (2005, p. 112). Reason (2007) suggests that a critical examination of Whiteness will never be achieved without White people being able to rearticulate what Whiteness means, a major focus of our chapter–re-articulating or repositioning the hook. Applebaum (2007) attempts to make sense of what it means when White peoples believe that they do not recognize or attach meaning to race, and articulates that "before social justice educators can contemplate what to do to promote student engagement, they must consider what is supporting student disengagement," particularly as it relates to race, racial identity, and Whiteness (p. 465).

Exploring the less virulent but equally disturbing, perplexing, and problematic forms of Whiteness and racism has not been a priority within society, particularly within the academy, and has become less of a priority in the so-called "post-racial Obama era" (Clark, Fasching-Varner, and Brimhall-Vargas, 2012). Consequently, the property value of less virulent White racists is often left without interrogation, remains unexamined, and, therefore, is fully maintained. In our chapter, our perspectives are situated around disrupting the value of Whiteness while also more expansively examining and situating our Whiteness so as to be responsible for the consequences of our Whiteness as members of the academy.

METHODOLOGICAL APPROACH

Who We Are and the Contexts in Which We Work?

To introduce you to the chapter authors, prior to sharing our narratives, we want to briefly highlight who we are in author order.

Kenny has spent his 13-year career working first in elementary, bilingual, special education for four years, and then in higher education in urban settings for nine years in New York, Ohio, Wisconsin, and now Louisiana. Kenny holds dual citizenship with the United States and Germany, and he grew up in a working-class household. Despite being from an immigrant family of low-socioeconomic status, Kenny was socialized around White privilege and racist narratives promoted from within his family. In his own K-12 experiences, Kenny attended public schools in a community whose narrative about public education was negative and problematic, particularly as it related to the community's racialized narratives. After completing his teaching certificate, he returned and taught in the same school system where he was educated, committed to disrupting the narratives that the community had about students and families within the district.

Margaret-Mary is a literacy educator who has had an extensive 33-year career in public K-12 education in Iowa, Minnesota, Mississippi, and Louisiana. The daughter of Croatian and German immigrants, Margaret-Mary grew up in a privileged, upper-middle-class household and attended private Catholic schools. In her own K-12 experiences, especially in her home state of Iowa, the power positioning of Whiteness was accepted both in her home and within the public school system where she chose to work. Although she was sensitive to her parents' status as immigrant

Americans, growing up in Waterloo, Iowa she also tacitly understood the issues surrounding race. She came more fully to understand Whiteness during her fifteen-year career teaching in the Waterloo, Iowa public schools, a system with a diverse student population compared to the almost exclusively White student population in the Catholic system that educated her. Her perceptions of Whiteness were exacerbated upon moving to the South 13 years ago, first to Hattiesburg, Mississippi as an Assistant Professor, then serving as a district assistant superintendent in Baton Rouge, home to the longest continuously-litigated desegregation case in the nation.

Dana is a former physical education teacher and administrator at both the school and district level who is from the Pacific Northwest and spent a significant amount of time in the West Mountain region. In her own K-12 experiences growing up in Eugene, Oregon, she rarely experienced diversity, attending White suburban neighborhood public schools composed of student from middle-class and upper-middle-class White families. As a teacher and school/district administrator for 28 years, she found that experiences with diversity did surface, yet working in a suburban school district limited her engagement with diversity to the same magnitude as might have occurred in many urban settings.

Steve is an English educator from the West Coast and Mountain West region of the U.S. He spent his formative years in Las Vegas attending schools that, while integrated, were academically tracked, leaving students of different races to mingle in the arts, gym, and vocational classes. He was aware of his Whiteness as a privileged position. Steve has worked in public education his entire career in Utah and now in Louisiana teaching grades 9–12, working with every ability group. Steve perceives himself as an active Mormon who votes for Democrats and lives with the apparent incongruity.

Kenny, Margaret-Mary, Steve, and Dana, have approximately 80 combined years of experience working in and with K-12 public education.

Data Sources

Within the research fields of anthropology, sociology, and education, ethnographic researchers typically study "others"; however, within autoethnography, self-study provides a method to situate data in sociocultural, historical, political, and personal contexts (Reed-Danahay, 1997). In autoethnographic research, the individual(s) reporting becomes the core and focus of the research (Ellis, 2004; Ellingson, 1998; Jackson, 1989; Tedlock, 1991): "Autoethnography is part *auto* or self and part *ethno* or culture" (Ellis, 2004, p. 31). Autoethnography seemed a particularly appropriate tool for interpreting our experiences with Whiteness from our personal perspectives and for sharing our stories. As Ellis has suggested, "stories are the way humans make sense of their world" (2004, p. 32). Our stories became the narratives for this chapter and, thus, our primary data source.

Constructing Narratives

To construct our narratives for this chapter, we first met as a group to discuss the call for chapters and what our approach might be. By sharing and charting our experiences, we quickly agreed that "unhooking" from Whiteness would not be a feasible approach, given the nature of how we are privileged by Whiteness and the racism attached to Whiteness. Consequently, we wanted to cast a critical self-reflexive gaze on our work to keep steadfast in our minds that Whiteness has had a prominent and, at times, quite problematic presence in our work. To engage with the exercise of dismantling racism, we wanted to constantly remind ourselves and one another how often the racism of Whiteness is automatically operationalized in our lives.

As a second step in generating the narratives—our data—after our initial meeting, we wrote each one separately. Next, we shared our stories electronically, with each of us providing critical feedback to one another. This was a recursive process where we asked each other clarifying questions and probed the significance of our individual narratives. After this virtual feedback, each of us re-examined our narrative attempting to tell clear and coherent a story as possible. With each narrative we attempted to unpack the Whiteness concurrently to some extent. We met again after receiving initial editorial feedback and re-examined our narratives through a CRT lens. This led to a final round of self-critique wherein we once again examined how our personal experience impacted us as individuals, as teacher educators, and as scholars within our fields of study.

From the outset, we want to highlight that these autoethnographic narratives are at best partial and subjective and not meant to reveal how we came to realize we were White or racist; these narratives are meant to show that despite differences in our identities and experiences, Whiteness has played such a predominant role that we consciously have to articulate the way Whiteness hooks, reifying privilege for some and marginalization for others. That is, the narratives in themselves can never represent the totality of even a single experience, and surely do not comprehensively address the full nature of Whiteness in our lives. When reading these narratives, it may be helpful to think of your own autoethnographic narratives and how they might contribute to the act of dismantling racism.

THE NARRATIVES

Kenny

I attended Breezy Middle School, a large urban middle school, with approximately 2,000 students. Despite my work with racial identity as an academic, my denial of issues surrounding race and ethnicity facilitated my spending little time or attention on my experiences of younger years. I have, however, been confronted with situations that illuminated my own struggle with my White supremacy/racism and, consequently, my White racial identity. These were incidents that I (sub)consciously denied to protect my self-image as a good, rational, non-judgmental person.

One such instance happened several years ago, when I taught a course called "Diversity, Social Justice, and Education" at Ivoryville College. I organized the course around the interrelated concepts of equity, understanding self, and interrogating dominant discourses. My orientation in preparing the course is ironic given what occurred.

On the first night of the class I was confronted by my racism when, during a break, a young woman said in disbelief, "You don't remember who I am, do you? "Did you go to Breezy?"

I responded that I did.

Ana proceeded to tell me, "I really don't know how I can take this course with you—it's pretty messed up really that *you* of all people would be teaching a course in diversity; I was in your class and we both applied to go to Unique High (UH), and we both got interviewed. I got in and you didn't. You and the other two White boys that didn't get in tormented me for the rest of the school year. The last month of school was awful, and you said that I only got in to UH because I was Hispanic and that hard working people like you get punished for being White."

As recognition slowly dawned, memories I had repressed of my own youthful behavior began to nudge at the edges of my consciousness. I felt my throat constrict and my pulse kick up. Embarrassed, I began to stammer a reply, but she was not finished.

Squaring her shoulders, she pressed on. "You told me if acceptance was based on work quality and intelligence you should be going there and not me. I will never forget those words! The words you and those other boys used haunted me all four years at UH – I always asked myself, why am I here, did I not deserve to be here? Now you are supposed to teach me about diversity, and your whole talk about getting to know yourself—it all seems like crap; you don't even know who you are. How could you forget the way you treated me?"

UH was vastly different from other schools. Students had the freedom to come and go as they pleased, eat meals in classes, call teachers by first names, and the school was exempt from state testing. There was a lengthy interview process to gain admission. The myth was that UH used racial and ethnicity quotas, and that of the 40 new freshman students only a few would be White and male. What I now know is that the school took the students who, during the interview process and based on teacher recommendation and interviews, were best suited to the school—I was not chosen, and Ana was.

Kenny's Analysis

After her initial confrontation, I recalled the events and put together the pieces. A numb feeling ran through my body. I remembered articulating all the ideas that Bonilla-Silva (2006) identifies as being color-blind and based in false sense of merit. I was the child of an immigrant; my mother spoke English as a second language; I could have and should have been a different person. In our house, however,

Whiteness took precedence. My mother actively refused to teach me German, and I could be "read" or perceived for what I was—White—with all the privileges that are associated with Whiteness. I had no basis to judge Ana or to think that she was less deserving than I was to attend Unique High. Ana was more deserving to go there since she was chosen, and I was not. The White supremacy, racism, and stereotypes about minorities that I had been socialized to believe created a situation where my Whiteness was directly lodged as a weapon against Ana. It forced me to acknowledge that, at best, I could be an anti-racist racist (Clark & O'Donnell, 1999). Despite my theoretical understandings of race, diversity, and multiculturalism, I had not done the basic reflective work necessary to understanding my own Whiteness in a meaningful way. If I were to continue to see myself merely as an anti-racist, I would keep doing the work that Ana intuitively understood to be hypocritical—telling teachers to do things I was not willing or able to do myself.

Ana helped me to understand the shortcomings of the White racial identity model's linear progression. Ana was, consequently, exploited by me for the second time in her life. Painfully, my learning came at the social cost of her having to take a class in anti-oppressive education from one of the very people who had oppressed her.

Ana and I discovered a number of anomalies in our experiences highlighting the tangible effects of racism. I became fluent in Ana's native language of Spanish, living in Spain and Chile, whereas Ana explained that she lost a lot of her Spanish because she was socialized to believe—by the actions of my White racism and that of others—that her Spanish was not a valued commodity, rather, a marker of difference used to judge her. Ana finished high school and went to college, feeling that she always had to prove herself to White people because there was an undercurrent form of narrative that someone was always judging her and believing that she did not deserve to be there. On the other hand, I flourished in college, to a large extent just by being White, quickly learning to manipulate my Whiteness for its benefits in negotiating relationships with professors. I was also able to manipulate my working-class upbringing as a means of receiving sympathy from faculty, all the while hiding behind my privilege.

I went on to teach children and then to educate future teachers on how to do "the work" I had yet to do myself. I eventually focused my studies on CRT and multiculturalism to compliment my literacy background, hoping to prepare teachers to better serve populations who have received the least from the educational system. Ana, meanwhile, entered a career in social work and saw how children from her Latino community in Lilac were being mistreated by a predominately White teaching force and community bent on punishing children and families of color. Ana wanted to protect students of color, from people like me—the Kenny whose Whiteness, along with other White people, helped to shape two distinct trajectories. This experience was not the first time I realized that I was White, racist, or privileged—but this experience has served to keep my Whiteness in check and at the forefront of my mind so that I work against racism and privilege despite being on Whiteness' hook.

Margaret-Mary

Who you are, your background, and your experiences will probably color your reaction to this vignette. You might be just as perplexed as I was by a question posed by a former student, or you just might wonder what was wrong with me, *that* teacher, on a wintry Iowa afternoon so long ago.

Almost 20 years ago, a young girl named Natalie taught me a great language lesson and a great lesson about Whiteness and racism. Natalie was a vivacious fifth grader and a stellar student. She loved to learn, she was social and outgoing, and she was becoming an avid writer. In short, she expressed herself well and had newly discovered the power of the written word.

Natalie's family had been members of the Great Migration, an internal migration wherein significant numbers of Southern Blacks left the South for points west, east, and north (Grossman, 1989). Natalie's family had arrived in Waterloo, Iowa, my hometown, in the early 1900's from rural Holmes County, Mississippi. Coming from rural Mississippi, Natalie's family retained a home language that scholars such as Baugh (1983), Dillard (1972), Labov (1972; 1982), Rickford (1999), Rickford & Rickford (2000), and others termed BEV or Black English.

My family arrived from Eastern Europe a few decades after the Great Migration, by way of Chicago, and then southern Iowa. Although Croatian was my father's home language, and my mother's was German, as children we acquired the more common midland vernacular dialect of most White people who live in the Midwest. Like Kenny, as a child, I was expected to speak English....*good* English, what some refer to as standard English.

By 1993, I had been in the classroom for almost fifteen years, and I prided myself on being a smart, informed, experienced teacher. In fact, I had just begun my doctoral degree and was quite confident about what I knew. Natalie reminded me of how far I had to go.

As she sat writing in my class one wintry December afternoon, she looked up and asked me, "How do you spell <u>which</u>?" In my best teacher manner—or so I thought—I probed, "<u>Which</u> as in <u>which</u> one do you want, or <u>witch</u> as in the women who wear black and ride on brooms?"

Expectantly, I waited for her to clarify, so I could try to guide her to a standard spelling of the word she wanted, the right way. I remember thinking how clever I was to quickly state two perfect examples of what I thought was right.

Natalie cocked her head and stared at me for a moment with a look of utter amazement and then slowly said, "<u>Which</u> as in what's the matter <u>which</u> you?"

She put her pen down, crossed her arms and waited for my response.

I started back with my mouth hanging open, but I recovered quickly and gently said, "Oh, that <u>which</u> is actually spelled <u>w-i-t-h</u>."

"But why?" she asked earnestly. "I don't say it that way. Madda fact, nobody in my house talks that way. Sometimes I say <u>wit</u> and for me, it means the same thing."

Twenty-five years later, I vividly remember her intent look and her keen desire to know why. Natalie and I spent the next several minutes discussing how a word is spelled versus how it might sound and why some folks say a word one way, yet others would say the same word differently—why she and I said this word differently. I told her I talked like my brothers and sisters, but not so much like my mom, dad, or grandparents. We explored some differences, like wit, which and with, and simply talked about language. Thinking back, I hope I was diplomatic and displayed finesse. For me, this was one of the most profound conversations I have had about language, teaching, writing, and spelling, and I had that conversation with a fifth grader. I still remember her earnestness, her desire to do it right, for me, her teacher. I also still remember her wonderment at my lack of understanding of her language.

Margaret-Mary's Analysis

According to Hilliard (1996), Delpit (1995), and Hale-Benson (1986), a huge mismatch can and often does occur when educators lack the knowledge, understanding, and acceptance of their students' language and culture, especially when it differs from their own. What happens, then, to children who are raised with one language system but schooled in another? How do children maneuver in U.S. society with a home language that differs significantly from the mainstream majority? Who helps the child mediate or navigate between two worlds? More importantly, how does a White, middle-income, female teacher—our nation's majority teaching force—address linguistic difference in the classroom? As a teacher educator, how can I reposition the hook?

Now and then, I think back on the situation and am appalled at my own ignorance, my superiority, and I am furious at myself for the way I handled the incident. My lack of knowledge about and understanding of Natalie's language confounded me. I felt defeated, then and even now, like I had somehow let Natalie down.

When thinking about my Whiteness, the concept of being like a traveler in a foreign land emerges. It is easy to remain in a place where one is comfortable, but that place does not give you opportunities to experience new things, or to grow. As a traveler, one takes in new experiences, reflects on those moments against the backdrop of other life events, and grows in new ways. In this exchange with Natalie I began a journey of understanding, acceptance, and knowledge around my Whiteness. This personal journey is one that I am still traveling, and while unhooking from my Whiteness may not be a goal, experiences like the one I had with Natalie help create a vigilance about how Whiteness operates. Natalie taught me that there is no "one language" of expression, that how I stated or voiced something had no more or less meaning than her manner of expression. In fact, I now view Natalie as having superior language skills because she was able to mediate two language worlds: the one of her upbringing, and the world of school. While unhooking from my Whiteness may not have been possible or even a desirable goal when this conversation occurred, reflexively examining my experiences provides a space for helping me to dismantle racism in my own and others' work. My ways of expression are just that: my way of speaking; they are no better than any other way of speaking. As I live and work in Louisiana, I often think of Natalie and how a single conversation allowed me to examine my own views of language, superiority, and, ultimately, Whiteness. I wish she could see how I have grown as an educator, how I no longer label language as right or wrong, how I simply focus on a speaker's meaning above all else. I wish I could tell her that I'm not as ignorant and superior these days, and that I have shed some of my own White privilege, especially as it relates to language. And I wish I could tell her how she taught me a lesson about Whiteness, a lesson that permeates my thoughts about Whiteness.

"Hey Natalie," I want to say, "I understand myself a little better now. My way isn't the only way, and it never was the 'right' way."

Dana

Often, I feel like an imposter when I face the educational leadership cohorts that I currently teach in South Louisiana. My work is to prepare practicing teachers to lead schools as principals. Most of these aspiring principals currently work in high poverty urban and rural schools, with the Black student populations approaching 90%. Most will start their administrative careers in these settings. Yet I stand before each group as a White middle-class female with no administrative experience in urban, high-poverty schools with primarily minority student populations. An imposter? My 16 years as a school and district administrator seem to provide me with credibility in the eyes of these future principals. Do I tell them that this experience should be discounted in light of my lack of personal experience with their contexts? Or, do I use that credibility to advance what I have learned from my vicarious experiences reading, researching, and observing classrooms and schools in high poverty, high minority settings? Obviously, they see my Whiteness, but do they also see my doubt? I question my understanding of what it is like to live and work with poverty. I question my own White privilege, which colors my understanding of the contextual nature of schools impacted by high poverty. I question my understanding of the day-to-day grind of working under the stress of accountability, where principals will be fired for not closing the "achievement gap." One moment I resolve that I am providing these aspiring principals with the knowledge, skills, and dispositions that will help them successfully lead these challenging schools. The next moment, I am confronted with a question or situation posed by a cohort member that shakes my confidence.

My own inner battle is compounded by the Whiteness and culture these aspiring principals bring to the cohort. At best, 20% of each cohort is composed of Black aspiring principals. Through the lenses of their (racial) backgrounds, cohort members often express views that are in contrast to my cognitive understanding of effective leadership in high impact schools. The life experiences and examples they bring to cohort discussions are, often, out of my practical frame of reference. I have not personally experienced the depth, volume, and intensity of the racial and cultural issues that these teachers and their principals face in their schools. Though I know I should challenge some of the conceptions and solutions cohort members express in our work together, I frequently question how practical my "theoretical" guidance might be in the context of their experiences. Do I really understand the complex, divergent, and overlapping cultural perspectives these teachers bring to their work in schools?

I juxtapose this inner conflict with a situation that recently occurred in class. The topic was the importance of parental engagement in student outcomes and school improvement. Research and theory would overwhelmingly suggest that engaging parents in a two-way dialogue while supporting family involvement in schools not only builds school-home ties and a positive culture, but improves student outcomes (Sheldon & Epstein, 2004; Sheldon & Epstein, 2002). My own professional experience and the parent-engagement literature suggest parents do want their children to succeed and do have positive aspirations for their children (Spera, Wentzel, & Matto, 2009). Further, it is the school administrator who has the greatest impact on culture as the principal involves the school community in the development of school expectations and structures that support parent engagement (Leithwood, Louis, Anderson & Wahlstrom, 2004).

With that in mind, I made the statement, "Not that it couldn't happen, but in 28 years as a teacher and administrator, I have never met a parent that didn't love their child and want them to succeed. Sometimes parents just don't know how to support them in schools." Stereotypes are false and harmful because they paint with a broad brush, categorizing everyone in a particular group (be it race, gender, ethnicity, etc.) according to a single, simple caricature. Statistically speaking, though, there will inevitably be someone who does "fit" or align with the stereotype. Undoubtedly the story this cohort member shared did happen (unless she had some reason to make it up). The failure here on the part of some of the cohorts would be to take a single anecdote and apply it broadly, to assume it is the rule and not the exception.

A White cohort member commented about one of her Black high school student's parents: "I have. The parent said to me she wished her child had never been born. She wished she didn't have to take care of him, and the kid was sitting right next to her." This statement reinforced what the literature suggests is a stereotypical belief by teachers that poor Black parents don't care (Spera, Wentzel, & Matto, 2009). Equally reinforcing was the fact that no one in the cohort challenged her. In fact, one of the Black students and a couple of cohort members affirmed by nodding their heads. There I was, exposed. What do I say? With all my administrative background and education, I did not know and could not know the experiences faced by these future administrators. I questioned myself. How do I debunk the myth and still maintain credibility for future discussions if I have not stood face-to-face with these realities? I even thought, "Is this a stereotype or is this the reality, that there are parents who do not care?" I struggled, but I also remained silent, and let the stereotype continue. I hung onto my Whiteness.

While this inner battle was raging, I was also replaying a past dissonant conversation that occurred in one of my doctoral classes 8 years earlier. The class topic was critical race theory and post colonialism. That day I sat next to Terri, a Black colleague with whom I had worked on a project in a previous class. White privilege was the topic of discussion when a White student in the class made a comment about how empathy was one solution to the issues among race and culture. Terri, a normally passive participant in class, sat up in her chair and with an aggressive demeanor stated, "You can empathize all you want, but you will never know what it is like to be Black. You will never know what small and large indignities and experiences have led to how I see the world."

I remember there being an uncomfortable pregnant pause in class. I do not remember what was said after that because I was embroiled in my own inner struggle. How can I/will I deal with understanding my experiences in relationship to working with students and colleagues of color and from diverse backgrounds? I really will never know what it is like to be Black, Hispanic, and so on. I can only try to unhook from my Whiteness.

All of this commotion was swirling around in my head as I tried to decide where to turn the class conversation. It was a double dilemma. I still struggle with my own Whiteness, and I was further struggling with my lack of experience in leading ethnically and culturally diverse schools. My reflection-in-action options for resolution were: (1) Take a power position and tell this aspiring principal, in a respectful, professional manner, that the research says she is wrong. The parent does care and the cohort is stereotyping. Then give her the litany of research that supports this position; (2) minimize the comment by stating this was probably an anomaly and move on with ideas of how to engage families in schools; (3) engage the class in a discussion of race, class, and stereotyping; (4) or expose myself as an imposter and tell them I don't know how to deal with Black families that live in poverty. Unbelievably, and luckily, it was the end of class, so I just postponed my decision—saved by the bell. I ended class with something like, "That is an interesting comment, and we will continue our discussion about family involvement next class."

Dana's Analysis

I pondered all week after that class session about my unresolved issues. I wondered about the notion of the imposter syndrome (Bell, 1995a; Bell 1995b). Is it possible to be a White imposter, believing that one is not adequate in dealing with diversity? I wondered about how to help my students to be culturally competent when I was so uncertain about my own competence. I wondered about how I would best deal with the low expectations and stereotyping these future leaders were supposed to correct and that seemed to be reflected in the comments about this one parent the previous week. I wondered if I had the courage to do anything at all.

My conclusions after a week of reflection-on-practice: honesty, courage, and openness should win out. I began the next class with, "I have been struggling all

83

week with a comment made by Susan last class. I appreciate how the topic made me confront my feelings, inadequacies, and inexperience." I shared what is written here with the class and we engaged in a lively discussion. Was this the best tact to take? Was my Whiteness unhooked, or did I just make more transparent how my Whiteness has allowed me to experience a different reality than those experienced by these students? I am not certain. This experience certainly did not resolve my issues. It perhaps helped me again to be much more cognizant of the routine need to continually trouble my own perceptions about race and the resulting actions I do or don't take; at least my hook of Whiteness was repositioned. Did these future school leaders change their dispositions, attitudes, and beliefs from this one dialogic experience? My impressions from the openness, tone, and tenor of the conversation indicated that, maybe, they began to question their own notions of race and class and how they will view the parents and students in their schools. Perhaps this is the best I can do as an imposter: create the dissonance and disruption that will help future administrators continually interrogate their own experiences and belief systems, in hopes that they lead other educators in efforts to dismantle the racism of Whiteness.

Steve

Two parallel concrete personal experiences, told through this single vignette, frame how I think about race in schools and my repositioning from the hook. In both instances I was a side participant in the conversation, but both replay in my mind during every conversation with pre-service teachers about race and diversity. Most of my students' field experiences and student teaching is in schools that are easily composed of 70% Black students. Generally, the classroom environments they experience are radically different from the ones they attended as White middle- and upper-class students. They are not only learning patterns of instruction, but are also learning about cultural differences, poverty, mandated curriculum, and tracking systems that often tend to further segregate schools. Both instances focus on a student's use of the term "colored people." One happened in the late spring of 1973 and the other in the spring of 2003. One might think that the term would not have surfaced again after thirty years, but there it was—out in the open all over again.

Visiting the Student Government Room

In 1973 I was a senior in high school in Las Vegas, Nevada. I attended a school that was about 70% White and 30% Black. During that decade African American wasn't the term that was in common use. The African American students were called Black, not Negro or colored.

The high school was built in 1963, and after some turbulent racial incidents during our sophomore and juniors years, the school was experiencing a slight racial renaissance. That year found the school with its first Black cheerleader and its first Black student body officer. I was the new student body president and the only White male on the student council; Alvin was the new second vice president and the only Black male. The five remaining members of the executive committee were White females who came into their office with experience in student government. Alvin and I were the newcomers, and most people were trying to figure out how we got there in the first place. Because of our novice status, we became allies in hostile territory as well as fast friends.

The year was full of new experiences or "firsts" for both of us. Alvin was the first Black person to give me a ride home from school, and I was the first White person to drop him off at his doorstep. We both knew we were out of place in each other's neighborhoods just as we were in the student government room. Both of us were figuring out what it meant to have a close association with a classmate from a different racial group. During class time we experienced different worlds given the organization of our class schedules. Our school lives intersected at extracurricular activities—dances, assemblies, and sporting events. We found that we spent more and more time together in the student government room before school, during lunch, and occasionally after school before various practices and activities.

During a lunch meeting, Alvin and I and one of the girls were planning an event that had long lost any importance when one of my friends bolted into the room. I am quite sure he expected to find me there, but not Alvin. Apparently, a serious fight had erupted down the hall near the cafeteria. Clint was already shouting that two colored kids were beating each other up. (Now, let's freeze the action as it must have been for Clint. He wasn't actually going to say colored at all, but rather a more offensive epithet. His mouth was running full speed as he saw Alvin sitting next to me— he was lucky to slide his tongue around a different label.) Alvin stared absolutely deadpan at Clint. The tension in the air was palpable. We knew that the N-word was beyond inappropriate and that "colored" just didn't work anymore—even if it had been used respectfully.

I watched as Alvin methodically shifted his six-foot three-inch frame forward in his chair. Without raising his voice, but moving in a way that manifested his full presence, he slowly asked a profound rhetorical question: "What color were they— purple?"

Clint just as slowly reflected on the question, fully knowing the answer, and quietly responded—"Black."

There was absolutely no doubt that the three White people in the room understood that the appropriate and preferred term of Alvin's generation was Black. After all, in 1968 James Brown began shouting over the radio, "Say it loud—I'm Black and I'm Proud." I was quite clear in understanding that I would never be in a position to define how members of another race would choose to define themselves. I try to remember that even when a White majority marginalizes the other by either practice or policy, those who are continually "othered" have the right to define themselves and insist on change. While I might not be able to unhook from Whiteness, I can maneuver and manipulate the power inherent in my Whiteness to open conversations and, more importantly, minimize my position while others speak for themselves and claim power and authority.

I went away to college and eventually took a job teaching in a predominantly White and homogenous school district. The high schools I taught in were quite different than the one I had attended. The minority students primarily consisted of small groups of Mexican-Americans, Native Americans, Vietnamese, Laotians, and Polynesians. It was 30 years after my high school graduation that I had another striking experience with the term. After more than twenty years teaching, I enrolled at the University of Georgia at Athens to pursue a degree in English education. As part of my training and assistantship I supervised student teachers in schools with highly "diverse" populations. Most of us in education realize that the term, "diverse" populations, is code for high minority populations (higher than the population rate nationwide), generally with significantly challenging economic positions. Given that definition, many of the schools I went to were more diverse than the school I attended, or the ones I worked in. Indeed, the statics were often the reverse of the 70% White to 30% Black ratio of the high school I attended. These schools also had several levels of tracking in most subject areas. The English departments had three groupings: Regular, College Preparation, and Advanced Placement.

Visiting Ms. Sackett

I arrived to observe Emily Sackett just before a class break. She was typical of the pre-service teachers in the program: young, White, and female. As the bell rang and students began leaving and others started to arrive, we chatted over a few details. I asked how she was doing, about her lesson planning, her classroom management, and her overall satisfaction with the experience. Emily was doing a tremendous job—her cooperating teacher thought she was doing well, she worked well with her students, and she was always ready to teach.

I complicated the observation a bit by asking one question too many about the next class. She explained that the next class was CP 12 English class, and I asked her to explain to me the real difference between a CP class and an AP class. I thought she might brush it to the side by saying something like—they have a rigorous curriculum but don't specifically prepare for the advanced placement exams. Emily, however, was quite astute; she knew exactly what the difference was. The class divisions functioned as a fairly strict tool for segregation. Her eyes scanned the room as it was beginning to fill up with students; she seemed to be wondering if there were just too many ears to explain to me what I already knew. As she searched for words one of the early arrivers, a young Black female student, decided to help her out. Janel was sitting fairly close to the front of the room where we were talking. And, yes, she had been listening. Full of adolescent energy she decided to help Miss Sackett. She entered into the conversation: "Miss Sackett, it's okay. You can tell him. Everybody knows that CP stands for the colored people class." The adults in the room, Emily and I, were momentarily frozen. A young adolescent had captured the tragic consequences of tracking and the unfortunate label.

Steve's Analysis

In both incidents, the White people in the room were uncomfortable and at a loss for words. On the other hand, in both cases the young Black adolescent knew exactly how the inadequacies of racist labels were being played out around them. I try to remember the power and courage that two young people demonstrated as they took over the conversation. Indeed, they controlled the labels that had been imposed on them. Alvin made it clear that if he were going to be reduced to a color it would be one he owned, one he was proud to wrap around his identity. It wasn't Clint's place, or mine, or any White person's for that matter, to define Alvin or his race. His confidence reminds me of the dignity that both of us were trying to master throughout that school year of change and challenge. And yes, Alvin had a more difficult time of it than I did, than I ever would. I followed in a pattern of White male student body presidents. He blazed a new path under scrutiny that I cannot even imagine. To do so would be to assume all of the privileges of Whiteness, and I cannot do that.

Janel, in her power move, sarcastically marginalized a class label that intentionally or not, was reduced to CP and consequently for "colored people." Since the CP classes successfully functioned as the default course for Black students, it didn't matter if it stood for college preparation. After talking with her, I discovered she planned on college, but she could not be bothered to strive for AP English, a class that obviously wasn't meant for her. She seemed determined to prepare herself where her friends were.

While the stories remain important reminders for me, I am not sure what they mean. Alvin certainly seemed more forceful and resolute than Janel, but much of that might have to do with gender, the social conditions of the time, and his position of power as a successful athlete and student leader. Janel was female and one of the many marginalized Black students in a school that had elite classes that housed the majority of the White minority. She was acknowledging the tragic fact that the integrated schools were still separate and still not equal. In part, each incident demonstrates that students have the ability to self-identify, by embracing a term as Alvin did or by sarcastically stating out loud and making transparent the racism that everyone knew was there as Janel did. What does it mean? It means that I tell the stories to the pre-service teachers in my classes and force conversation about our Whiteness and our racism—especially as we have experiences that expose the power and social privileges of that Whiteness.

WHAT DOES IT ALL MEAN AND WHAT ARE THE IMPLICATIONS FOR TEACHER EDUCATION?

To conclude, we offer some commentary about the larger effect of Whiteness as exemplified in the narratives. As a small collective of White academics sharing a common space in a large university, we are clearly all at different places personally and professionally. Despite our differences in gender, ethnicity, religion, socio-economic status, and age, the sharing of the vignettes makes us all aware of the complex nature of Whiteness, and the ways in which we are snared upon Whiteness' hook. As the vignettes highlight, even Whiteness is not a completely shared construct or experience; we do agree, however, that what is shared is our racial privilege, and the ensuing benefits of our White privilege. How we think, how we feel, and how we try to engage our students in discussions of Whiteness, privilege, and racism are all results of our Whiteness, experiences, and scholarly exploration of these issues.

We are many things. We are no longer as smug as Kenny was so long ago. We have learned from our experiences and our students as seen in Margaret-Mary's vignette. We are not the imposters that Dana fears. And we are not as uncomfortable, as Steve once was, when we hear certain labels, feeling paralyzed to confront racism. Yet we are all White and, we suspect, we are all racist, albeit racist anti-racists.

We appreciate that the scholars of color who contributed to this volume have a right to be unhooked from Whiteness, but as White people, we cannot unhook from our experiences of being White and the attached privilege and racism. We can, as we believe we all have, distance ourselves from racist language, attitudes, and practices. While we may not believe we can unhook from our Whiteness, we have become vigilant about the ways in which our Whiteness operates, and we can become active in the enterprise of working toward dismantling the racism of our Whiteness.

In this chapter we take the risk of misinterpretation. On one hand, our vignettes can be reduced in one's mind to naïve narratives of White academic that reposition or center Whiteness and consequently do not present anything new; on the other hand, we could be misinterpreted as taking an easy way out by suggesting that we think it is impossible to unhook from Whiteness.

Our stance is different from these two positions, however, in that we wish to make transparent that Whiteness is omnipresent within the United States landscape (and for that matter throughout many places in the world). As a result we are obligated to be clear about the nature of Whiteness' hook, and how racism and privilege are not simply behavior that so-called virulent racists (i.e. the Klu Klux Klan) engage in; racism and privilege are a part of all White peoples' experiences.

In the end we are left with many questions. Will engaging other White and Black students in our own stories reduce racism? Can we impact the majority of White pre-service and in-service teachers through our sharing of stories and experiences? Will the academy and society transcend its racist foundations? How might White academics be willing to think in more nuanced ways, through their own auto-ethnographic narratives, as a means of disrupting the racist mantle of Whiteness?

These questions all require continued thought and reflection. Additionally these questions require action. As authors of this chapter, our hope is to encourage other White academics to push themselves in the same ways that our narrative inquiry presented in this chapter pushed us.

REFERENCES

Applebaum, B. (2007). White complicity an social justice education: Can one be culpable without being liable. *Educational Theory, 57*(4), 453–467.

Baugh, J. (1983). *Black street speech*. Austin, TX: University of Texas Press.

Bell, D. (1995a). Brown v. Board of Education and the interest convergence dilemma. In K.Crenshaw, N. Gotanda, G. Peller & K. Thomas (Eds.) *Critical race theory: The key writings that formed the movement* (pp. 20–28). New York, NY: The New Press.

Bell, D. (1995b). Racial realism. In K. Crenshaw, N. Gotanda, G. Peller & K. Thomas (Eds.) *Critical race theory: The key writings that formed the movement* (pp. 302–314). New York, NY: The New Press.

Carter, R. T., Helms, J. E., & Juby, H. I. (2004). The relationship between racism and racial identity for white Americans: A profile analysis. *Journal of Multicultural Counseling and Development, 31*(1), 2–17.

Clark, C., & O'Donnell, J. (1999). *Becoming and unbecoming white: Owning and disowning a racial identity*. Santa Barbara, CA: Praeger Press.

Clark, C., Fasching-Varner, K. J., & Brimhall-Vargas, M. (2012). *Occupying the academy: Just how important is diversity in higher education?* Landham, MD: Rowman & Littlefield.

Crenshaw, K. W. (1995). Race, reform, and retrenchment Transformation and legitimating in anti-discrimination law. In K. Crenshaw, N. Gotanda, G. Peller, & K. Thomas (Eds.) *Critical race theory: The key writings that formed the movement* (pp. 103–126). New York, NY: The New Press.

DeCuir, J. T., & Dixson, A. D. (2004). 'So when it comes out, they aren't that surprised that it is there': Using critical race theory as a tool of analysis of race and racism in education. *Educational Researcher, 33*(5), 26–31.

Delgado Bernal, D., & Villalpando, O. (2002). An apartheid of knowledge in academia: The struggle over the 'legitimate' knowledge of faculty of color. *Equity and Excellence in Education, 35*(2), 169–180.

Delpit, L. (1995). *Other people's children*. New York: The New Press.

Dillard, J. L. (1972). *Black English: Its history and usage in the United States*. New York: Random House.

Dixson, A. D., & Rousseau, C. K. (2005). And we are still not saved: Critical race theory in education ten years later. *Race, Ethnicity, and Education, 8*(1), 7–27.

Duncan, G. (2002). Beyond love: A critical race ethnography of the schooling of black males. *Equity and Excellence in Education, 35*(2), 131–143.

Ellingson, L. (1998). *Qualitative inquiry*. Thousand Oaks, CA: Sage Publications.

Ellis, C, (2004). *The ethnographic I*. Walnut Creek, CA: Alta Mira Press.

Fasching-Varner, K. J. (2009). No! The team ain't alright: The individual and institutional problematic of race. *Social Identities, 15*(6), 811–829.

Giroux, H. A. (1997). Rewriting the discourse of racial identity: Towards a pedagogy and politics of Whiteness. *Harvard Educational Review, 67*(2), 285–320.

Grossman, J. (1989). *Land of hope: Chicago, black southerners, and the great migration*. Chicago, IL: University of Chicago Press.

Hale-Benson, J. (1986), *Black children: Their roots, culture, and learning styles*. Baltimore, MD: A Johns Hopkins Paperback.

Hall, S. (1997). *Representation: Cultural representations and signifying practices*. Thousand Oaks, CA: Sage.

Harris, C. (1995). Whiteness as property. In K. Crenshaw, N. Gotanda, G. Peller & K. Thomas (Eds.) *Critical race theory: The key writings that formed the movement* (pp. 276–291). New York, NY: The New Press.

Hartigan, J. J. (1999). Establishing the fact of Whiteness. In R. D. Torres, L. F. Mirón, & J. X. Inda (Eds.) *Race, Identity, and Citizenship* (pp. 183–1999). Malden, MA: Blackwell Publishing.

Hartlep, N. D. (2012). *Going public: Critical race theory and issues of social justice*. Mustang, OK: Tate Publishing.

Hilliard, A. (1996). *The maroon within us: Selected essays on African American Community socialization*. Baltimore, MD: Black Classic Press.

Hurtado, A. (1999). The trickster's play: Whiteness in the subordination and liberation process. In R. D. Torres, L. F. Mirón, & J. X. Inda (Eds.) *Race, identity, and citizenship* (pp. 225–244). Malden, MA: Blackwell Publishing.

Ignatiev, N. (1995). *How the Irish became white.* New York, NY: Routledge.

Ignatiev, N. (1997a). Treason to Whiteness is loyalty to humanity. In R. Delgado & J. Stefanic (Eds.) *Critical white studies: Looking behind the mirror* (pp. 607–612). Philadelphia, PA: Temple University Press.

Ignatiev, N. (1997b). How to be a race traitor: Six ways to fight being white. In R. Delgado & J. Stefanic (Eds.) *Critical white studies: Looking behind the mirror* (p. 629). Philadelphia, PA: Temple University Press.

Jackson, M. (1989). *Paths toward a clearing: Radical empiricism and ethnographic inquiry.* Bloomington, IN: Indiana University Press.

Labov, W. (1972). *Language in the inner city studies in the black English vernacular.* Philadelphia, PA: University of Pennsylvania Press.

Labov, W. (1982). Objectivity and commitment in linguistic science: The case of the Black English trial in Ann Arbor. *Language in Society, 11,* pp 165–201.

Ladson-Billings, G. J. (1999). Just what is critical race theory and what's it doing in a nice field like education. In L. Parker, D. Deyhele & S. Villenas (Eds.) *Race is . . . race isn't: Critical race theory and qualitative studies in education* (pp. 7–30). Boulder, CO: Westview Press.

Ladson-Billings, G. J., & Tate, W. F. IV. (1995). Toward a critical race theory of education. *Teachers College Record, 97*(1), 47–68.

Leithwood, K. A., Louis, K. S., Anderson, S., & Wahlstrom, K. (2004). *How leadership influences student learning: Review of research* (Vol. 2006, pp. 1–90). Minneapolis; Toronto: Center of Applied Research and Educational Improvement, University of Minnesota; Ontario Institute for Studies in Education, University of Toronto.

Lemann, N. (1991). *The promised land: The great black migration and how it changed America.* New York: Knopf.

Lipsitz, G. (1998). *The possessive investment in Whiteness: How white people benefit from identity politics.* Philadelphia, PA: Temple University Press.

Lipsitz, G. (2005). Whiteness and war. In C. McCarthy, W. Crichlow, G. Dimitriadis, & N.Dolby (Eds.) *Race, identity, and representation in education* (pp. 95–115). New York, NY: RoutlegeFalmer.

Lipsitz, G. (2006). *The possessive investment in Whiteness: How white people profit from identity politics.* Philadelphia, PA: Temple University Press.

López, I. H. (2006). *White by law: The legal construction of race.* New York, NY: New York University Press.

Montague, A. (1997). *Man's most dangerous myth: The fallacy of race.* Walnut Creek, CA: Altamira Press.

Morrison, T. (1993). *Playing in the dark: Whiteness and the literary imagination.* New York, NY: Vintage.

Philipsen, D. (2003). Investment, obsession, and denial: The ideology of race in the American mind. *Journal of Negro Education, 72*(2), 193–207.

Reason, R. D. (2007). Rearticulating Whiteness: A precursor to difficult dialogues on race. *College Student Affairs Journal, 26*(2), 127–135.

Reed-Danahay, D. (1997). *Auto/ethnography: Rewriting the self and the social.* New York: Palgrave MacMillan, Ltd.

Rickford, J. (1999). *African American Vernacular English: Features, Evolution, Educational Implications.* Oxford, England: Blackwell Publishing.

Rickford, R. J., & Rickford, J. R. (2000). *Spoken soul: The story of black English.* Oxford, England: John Wiley and Sons.

Roediger, D. R. (1991). *The wages of Whiteness: Race and the making of the American working class.* London, GB: Verso.

Roediger, D. R. (1994). *Towards the abolition of Whiteness: Essays on race, politics, and working class history.* New York, NY: Verso.

Roediger, D. R. (1997). White looks: Hairy apes, true stories, and Limbaugh's laughs. In M. Hill (Ed.) *Whiteness: A critical reader* (pp. 35–46). New York, NY: New York University Press.

Roediger, D. R. (1998). *Black on white: Black writers on what it means to be white.* New York, NY: Schocken.

Roediger, D. R. (2004). Chinese immigrants, African-Americans, and racial anxiety in the United States 1848–82. *Journal of Social History, 37*(3), 802–8.

Sheldon, S., & Epstein, J. (2002). Getting students to school: Using family and community involvement to reduce chronic absenteeism. *The School Community Journal,* 39–56.

Sheldon, S. B., & Epstein, J. L. (2002). Improving student behavior and school discipline with family and community involvement. *Education and Urban Society, 35*(1), 4–26. doi: 10.1177/001312402237212

Sheldon, S. B., & Epstein, J. L. (2004). Getting students to school: Using family and community involvement to reduce chronic absenteeism. *School Community Journal, 14*(2), 39–56.

Smedley, A. (1998). "Race" and the construction of human identity. *American Anthropologist, 100*(3), 690–702.

Solorzano, D., & Yosso, T. (2002). Critical race methodology: Counter-storytelling as an analytical framework for education research. *Qualitative Inquiry, 8*(1), 23–44.

Spera, C, Wentzel, K. R., & Matteo, H. C. (2009). Parental aspirations for their children's educational attainment: Relation to ethnicity, parental education, children's academic performance, and parental perceptions of school climate. *Journal of Youth and Adolescence, 38,* 1140–1152.

Spera, C., Wentzel, K. R., & Matto, H. C. (2009). Parental aspirations for their children's educational attainment: Relations to ethnicity, parental education, children's academic performance, and parental perceptions of school climate. *Journal of Youth and Adolescence, 38*(8), 1140–1152. doi: 10.1007/s10964-008-9314-7

Tate, W. (1994). From inner city to ivory tower: Does my voice matter in the academy? *Urban Education, 29*(3), 245–269.

Tate, W., & Rousseau, C. (2002). Access and opportunity the political and social context of mathematics education. In L. English (Ed.) *Handbook of international research in mathematics education* (pp. 271–299). Mahwah, NJ: Lawrence Earlbaum.

Taylor, E. (2000). Critical race theory and interest convergence in the backlash against affirmative action: Washington state and initiative 200. *Teachers College Record, 102*(3), 539–560.

Tedlock, B. (1991). From participant observation to the object of the participant: The energy of narrative ethnography. *Journal of Anthropological Research, 41,* 69–94.

Winant, H. (2000). Race and race theory. *Annual Review of Sociology, 26,* 169–185.

MATTHEW WITT

7. ENGLISH IVY

Race for this country is like the thing in the story in the mythology for the kingdom to be well. And it [the thing] is always something that you don't want to do. And it's always that thing so much about you confronting yourself, that it's tailor made for you to fail dealing with it. And the question of your heroism and of your courage and of your success at dealing with this trial is: Can you confront it with honesty, and do you confront it and do you have the energy to sustain an attack on it? […] The more we run from it, the more we run into it. It's an age old story. If it's not race, it's something else. But in this particular instance, in this nation [United States], [this thing] is race.

—Wynton Marsalis (2000)

In order to get beyond racism, we must first take account of race. There is no other way. In order to treat some persons equally, we must treat them differently.

Supreme Court Justice Harry Blackmun (1978)

IF A RIBBON RAN THROUGH IT

Pondering how to draft this essay, I visualize the chronologies featured at the front end of *Everyman's Library* editions of great literature. Juxtaposed to major events of each author's life is the literary context, year by year, followed by major historical events, almost as if these concurrent moments were evident to the authors, themselves. Perhaps this is what Ralph Ellison or Harper Lee had in mind casting their monumental stories—*Invisible Man* and *To Kill a Mockingbird*, respectively— through the eyes of an omniscient narrator looking backward.

The *Everyman's Library* dignifies its venerable trove, and readers, with clothbound editions featuring a ribbon place mark. No amount of context will make what I have in mind producing here into great literature. Still, I wonder: If context was something any of us had in mind in any great measure from moment to moment, could we ponder our lives otherwise than in rearview? When it comes to context, the typical American educational experience defies a clear grasp of race dimensions. At best, we encounter this subject as if entering a house of mirrors, immediately beset by faceted, partial images of a radically fractured present tense, giving us as unclear a path forward as backward. This essay, in some ways inadvertently, is a testament to such lack of context, and a sacrament towards creating my own; towards making *myself* visible to myself and, for that matter, something other than a faceted, fractured

C. Hayes and N.D. Hartlep (Eds.), Unhooking from Whiteness:
The Key to Dismantling Racism in the United States, 93–101.
© 2013 Sense Publishers. All Rights Reserved.

reflection. In step with Gary Larson's famous *Far Side* cartoon featuring dinosaur in hot pursuit of motorist, I'm going to start with an object in my rearview mirror, now closer than it might otherwise appear. My thoughts then extend still further rearward. Harper Lee's semi-autobiographical, iconic character Scout of *To Kill a Mockingbird* would have me go back to Andrew Jackson. Wynton Marsalis might have me go further still. For present purposes, if I make it outside the mirrored house, I hope my effort will be sufficient.

COLORING OUTSIDE OF THE LINES

Countless classes and students later, my first full exposure to race in the classroom is as vivid to me now, years later, as it was then: There I am, standing in front of a classroom that 90 minutes earlier had been chatty and vivacious but now preternaturally quiet. Against my whiter impulses, I had scheduled for the class (upper division organizational behavior) to view the powerful documentary *The Color of Fear,* made in the wake of the riots responding to the Rodney King trial. I remember when I first saw it as a teaching assistant in graduate school. The film features a several-day encounter session between pairs of Black, White, Asian, and Latino men gathered together in Ukiah, California, moderated by an Asian-American therapist whose mother had been murdered in a robbery by a Black man. Each man's accounting of/with race is based on direct experience and personal reflection. The men gathered are articulate, introspective individuals, chosen as such by the therapist/moderator/producer of the film. The explosive climax builds as the first one among equally articulate men, one of the Black pair, engages the least introspective among the men, one of the white pair. Pain on all sides is exposed; provisional understanding is achieved. And as the film proceeds in my class that day, I sense around the room the soft shuffling of feet and arms withdrawing close into bodies. By the time the film ends, anticipation hovers in the air. I wasn't a teaching assistant anymore that day I showed the film to my class.

I suddenly realized that I had exposed these students, as if I had removed their clothing. *Oh no!* whispered my inner voice. Something had to be done quickly to restore a sense of collective modesty before the taboo topic of race was brought up. So I rose, walked up to the front of the class, scanned the souls gathered…and realized I was the most naked of all. Pondering my circumstance and searching for words appropriate to the moment, all I could produce was a slow motion "I…am… white," which tumbled forward from where I know not and by no conscious control, eliciting some knowing smiles and hushed tittering. Then came likewise "I…am… male," followed now by more open faces and relaxed laughter. About all I recall being aware of was not wanting to be the least introspective white person in the room.

Just a few weeks ago, a psychology colleague of mine mentioned he had heard someone in his department was considering showing *The Color of Fear* in a psychology class. This colleague rued plaintively what a mistake that would be.

I can't now recall his actual words, but I recall his affect. *That film* featured raw, exposed emotions on a matter he would not trust *ever releasing* into our campus climate. He spoke with the certainty that Ph.D.s sometimes speak indicating that further discussion is futile. I respect this colleague, and I doubt I have a sufficiently sophisticated response that would meet his high psychological standards for when and how race must be broached in the classroom.

How would my action appear to studious and cautious colleagues if they saw my gesture in that classroom in real time? Would I appear like a character from the science fiction film *The Matrix*, traversing sides of walls or suspended in thin air like an apparition warping space and time? Would they be spellbound, muttering "That's *impossible!*"? Would they have eyes to see or ears to hear my gesture at all? Do the rules governing "Whiteness" appear bendable to my learned colleagues? Perhaps seeing me in action they would morph suddenly into an Agent Smith, deployed to suppress any breach with the Matrix Code *Thou Shalt Not Question Too Deeply Race in America*. Maybe learned academic expertise is just another mystification of the canons of White privilege, available to shield us from encountering the dread at the center of *race* in America. Justice Blackmun's trenchant insight notwithstanding, White academics have all sorts of tricks for "getting past race." In my own experience (as with peer review), the "good liberals" among our tribe are the most loathe to fathom Blackmun's deceptive challenge, and for that matter are no less toxic than arch-conservatives to people of color navigating the matrix of White privilege in academia as professionals and students. Meanwhile, between unstudied daring and studied caution lies the vast uncharted terrain of race in America, and in my own life.

ORANGE, BLACK, AND IN BETWEEN

According to writing most influential on me, educators must strive to understand our own origins, influences, and outlooks; like psychiatrists, as it were, required to undergo analysis so that we don't inadvertently project subconscious fictions onto those we profess to teach. For me, this has required grappling with what is the ethnicity lurking behind my White*ness* and the (to White people) invisible privileges this otherwise incidental distinction confers. In this regard, a major influence, with which I am consciously familiar and will always struggle to really understand, is English Ivy.

When I was 6 years old, my parents moved us from a small Victorian, row-styled house to a large, craftsman-styled home a few blocks westward but still in Northwest Portland, on property that abutted the southeastern gateway to the largest continuous urban forested area in the country (over 5,000 acres), Forest Park. My twin brother and I would range across that park with friends over our formative years, mostly plying up the streambed, especially luring during winter time when the water often surged its banks and the ice-covered rocks. We would trudge that stream for hours a day, usually coming home just before nightfall, soaked to the bone. All over the banks of that stream, and up the steep slopes either side, there was English Ivy, in many instances climbing well up the trunks of second growth firs, alder, and birch populating the area. Sword Fern, indigenous to the acidic soil of that forest, was all but overrun by the shiny green leafy tentacles of English Ivy, which I would much later learn was an "exotic alien plant species" that would doom the forest if it was not eradicated.

As a child I was, of course, oblivious to this mortal threat to that which so enchanted and populated my imagination with countless Elysian fantasies, daydreams, and misty vistas. I was likewise unaware that this neighborhood I grew up in had been "red-lined" by mortgage banks years earlier because of plans to bulldoze a huge swath for freeway development, part of a scheme intended to transect Forest Park with freeway tentacles adjoining one interstate linkage to another. My parents and many among their professional and neighborly affiliations fought that freeway extension, and won. All that I was then dimly aware of was the industrial district that abutted the eastern edge of the park; forbidding territory my brother and I were not permitted to venture into: a stark, paved edge that would leach acrid fumes wafting just a bit into what was otherwise that enchanted forest.

Across the Willamette River from that industrial terrain was North and Northeast Portland, area that would be "red-lined" (unofficially) for decades longer because it was the depot for Portland's small Black population. When I was about 7 years old, my older sister became friends with a girl, Jackie, from the Albina district, center of Northeast Portland. On a few occasions over the next year, our families visited one another's homes. Still vivid to me are the impressions from those visits: Jackie's home was loud and boisterous and teeming with more than just immediate family members. Our home was quiet and subdued, rarely with more than immediate family. Jackie's home and street were filled with Black people old, young, and not so young; with music and food I did not know. Our home, and neighborhood, was exclusively white, filled then mostly with 40-something parents and their children spanning the late end and other side of the Baby Boom. Our home and neighborhood were surrounded by a lot of mature trees, and on the edge of a forest park. Jackie's neighborhood had very few trees. I recall the sun gleaming sharp and hot off worn asphalt surfaces and heat-ravaged grass lawns.

My brother and I were the youngest of 5 children of a half-Jewish immigrant mother from Nazi Germany who left at 17 in 1947, vowing never to return (but would, visiting her parents) and a Dustbowl-displaced father, himself with Cajun, Cherokee, and Virginian White-indentured heritage. One way or the other, our clan was the product of diaspora, flung to the northwestern-most corner of the northwestern-most neighborhood of the northwestern-most city of the (nearly) northwestern-most state of the Union; our backs eventually up against English Ivy swooping down upon us from the west, of all places. Jackie's family was surrounded by tentacles, too, only her family was very aware of how such binds confined them. We were not so aware, because we *were* the tentacles. Except for a smidge of Cherokee, we were White, *and how*.

Our clan on my father's side had extended itself across countless pasture and prairie acreage, finding itself—so it seemed to them and us—more by accident than providence in the Pacific Northwest, settling there rather than suffer the grapes of wrath that so many dustbowl families otherwise endured; for my father's parents were determined to avoid the depredations they heard awaited those lured to California when, in 1937, my grandparents reckoned their family had endured one sandstorm enough after my grandfather's small battery rebuilding business was by then bankrupted by the Depression.

When I was maybe 4 years old, I had my first encounter with Blackness. Viola, newly from Alabama, came to clean a house my parents had purchased for fix-up and rental. (Growing up on a small farm and serving as a carpenter's mate in the Navy, my father knew how to fix up anything made from wood; sweat equity was the only equity my parents had back then.) On one of these occasions, I sat beside Viola at kitchen table, chirping as I pointed to her darkly complected forearm, "Look Mommy, black!" This immediately elicited a terse response from an indignant Viola: "Don't you *ever* say black!!" According to my mother, I collapsed immediately into teary supplication, "Is it alright to say orange?" Orange and black were at the time my favorite colors. Black*ish* was the skin tone of my mother's first best American friend in Chicago where she attended the University of Chicago. My mother was never fully aware of American-style racism until that friend was denied invitation my mother had received to a swimming-pool gathering. In those days, my mother never, ever revealed her Jewish origins—to her the most dangerous thing she could do—anywhere. To her, survivor of Nazi plagued Germany, no stigma stained like being Jewish. Much later my mother would recall a Jewish acquaintance of her kin in New York speaking about the Black experience in America relative to Jews. In that interrogatory idiom that is uniquely Jew*ish*, this man uttered: "Is it so wrong that someone else is abused?"

When I was in graduate school for urban studies, I experienced one of my first adult intellectual epiphanies, or so it felt at the time: Race is the secret answer, and question, at the center of all problems, and solutions in America. This was hardly an original insight, except for another facet of relevance to my awareness about diversity: the graduate program in which I completed my degree, otherwise acclaimed as one of the best urban studies and planning programs in the country, had (at that time in the 1990s) virtually no curriculum explicitly dealing with how racism has indelibly shaped American cities. Various euphemism was permitted utterance in classes, such as oblique reference to "institutionalized racism" and a mysteriously, entrenched "dual housing market." But explicit questioning on the matter elicited mostly blank and sometimes taciturn stares. It was all right to say orange, as it were.

As for English Ivy, when I served as a neighborhood association board member for Portland's Northwest District Association during my stint in graduate school, I voted more than once to provide funding to the "No Ivy League," a grant funded initiative to purge Forest Park of its alien, invasive vine species. My stint as neighborhood association member eventually led to my decision for a dissertation topic, a chronicle of Portland's then 26-year history of formalized (city subsidized, authorized, and enfranchised) neighborhood organizing program. *No Ivy League* is an appellation limning notes deeper inside me than I had at the time made full acquaintance with. And anyone familiar with English Ivy knows how incredibly tenacious is its grip on vulnerable terrain, sinking deep taproots every few feet that are like earthen tapeworms.

In the years since I started working full time teaching, I have had countless encounters with diversity in classrooms at the University of La Verne, a Hispanic Serving Institution by federal designation (40% of our undergraduate student body is Hispanic affiliated, 40% White, 10% Black, 10% Asian and other). Countless times I have awkwardly attempted to elicit discussion on race; countless times I have felt the stern glare of every kind of student wishing I do otherwise. Say orange, say anything else. Just don't say "race." My students are very mixed age cohorts. Older students are generally more hesitant discussing race matters. But younger students too often confuse temporal propinquity with actual/real propinquity. Twitter and texting and the internet distort these relevant distinctions. I remind them that, geographically speaking, America is more race segregated today along White-Black lines than it was in 1950. "Huh?"

So I have persisted, and with some success I have managed to bring matters of race and diversity to the center of most of my teaching. Doing so has been an often exhausting challenge for me, and my students(!) How I have done so is a matter more of trial and error than any particular doctrine or technique; more a matter of stubborn determination than any artfulness. More than once, feeling myself aware I was more a fan dancer obscuring how naked I actually felt than any kind of "sage on the stage," I have retreated into memory that otherwise eluded me for years.

I grew up before TV colonized so many rooms of so many American homes. For that matter, dinner time when I grew up was family time, wedged between school for kids, dawn to dusk work for parents, and nighttime homework and bed. And dinner time was discussion time, usually conducted by my father at the head of the table, my mother chiming in regularly. For as many years as I can remember, discussion at dinner was not merely permitted; it was expected. And the discussion could range to any topic with the one condition that everyone was included one way or the other. Whatever you had to say it had better be in some way either funny, entertaining, or informative. Experiences that were only/merely personal were not pertinent topics unless there could be coaxed from them some kernel of shared relevance, insight, humor, etc. I'm pretty sure that what my dad had in mind was a kind of radically discursive democracy; some distant echo of his Oklahoma, Cherokee, radically populist roots that he shared in common with the kin of Will Rogers, Woody Guthrie et al. What actually occurred at our dinner table may have tended to favor (privilege) male boisterousness and showing off, but even for that: every kid in the family could mouth off so long as doing so touched on some kind of civic theme covering a broader spectrum than orange. For all of this discourse, it seemed to me my father variously aped Dean Martin, Budd Abbott or (a knock off) Socrates, goading the rest of us along.

In the classroom I have become my father more than once, coaxing and cajoling, ribbing and side-eyeing my students. From that permission granted me at the dinner table so long ago, I try to disclose something about myself in the process; show my students that I am forever recovering from my privileges, and that, for the moment, anyway, I am *among* them, *of* them, *with* them. Race is illusion; there is no scientific basis whatsoever vesting the construct any glint of legitimacy. But race is a brutal illusion; it is an alchemy that is at the center of American self concept; an illusion that scuttles consciousness and memory and undermines genuine kinship and intellectual integrity. "Skin tone is, fundamentally, a function of melanin production" I have sometimes been reduced to sputtering; because fighting this illusion is no option, for genuine "diversity" is meaningless without first grappling with the (almost entirely) self-unexamined, sublimated privilege that White*ness* confers. And because no privilege called a privilege is much of a privilege, the riddle at the center of the paradox of America is like a Mobius strip, forever turning in upon itself. It's no accident that so much of our popular comic culture is standup: talk is cheap in this land. And being cheapened, it is province for comic, and also tragic, parlay. Parlay is something I learned at a young age at the family dinner table; actualizing this in the classroom is not a straight line affair, for doing so risks eliciting psychological projection that is not as easily metered as is black from orange. But this is the best I have learned to do; for if I am not myself willing to model all the ambivalence and morbid dread that accompanies the descent into the realm of race in America, I cannot claim any real relevance to my students. I might as well otherwise be orange.

REAL TIME

The semester is wrapping up as this piece goes to press. Tomorrow evening is the last class of an ethics and leadership course I teach for the masters of public administration program. This term we have viewed part three, "The Houses We Build," of the documentary *Race: The Power of an Illusion*, and a lecture by Claude Steele on YouTube that synopsizes research on stereotype threat. Before this material, the students viewed the classic film *Twelve Angry Men*, which features jury deliberation following the sham trial of a non-White youth facing the death sentence for alleged first degree murder of his father. This morning, listening to the Pacifica Radio daily broadcast of *Democracy Now!*, I heard a taped recording of a lecture recently given by Michelle Alexander at the Abyssinian Baptist Church in Harlem. Alexander's recent book *The New Jim Crow: Mass Incarceration in the Age of Color Blindness* is being heralded as a major work of social history and policymaking. I found the recording on YouTube and saw Alexander speaking, full throated, in her presentation to an exclusively Black audience. This might not do for class, I reasoned. I looked for other segments and found some hour-long material that would test the patience of my Twitter-conditioned students. I found another segment on *Democracy Now!*, about 10 minutes, pitched to a key that my class will be able to "hear, together."

At a penultimate scene in the film *Twelve Angry Men*, Juror 8 (played by Henry Fonda, who produced the film) makes a final round of holdout jurors who, despite overwhelming evidence exculpating the young suspect of the alleged crime, refuse to concede a "not guilty verdict." Fonda challenges one of them, "Isn't it *possible* he's not guilty?" No, responds the one juror. Fonda marches to another. "Is it possible?" This juror—the most obviously racist of the three holdout jurors—is seated off to the side, dejected after venting a racist tirade and being told by another of the holdout jurors to shut his mouth and not speak again. Nodding his head in dejection, he mutters, "Not guilty."

And now I visualize two students in my class who have sat next to one another all term, a 20-something Black male and a 30-something White male. The White male is a sheriff's deputy, bright and articulate, reserved and measured in his remarks in class, who bears passing resemblance to the actor Martin Milner of the 1960s police series, *Adam 12*. The Black male has spoken in class very rarely, but has approached me on a few occasions with side remarks and questions about class, eyeing me cautiously. I have noticed both these men on occasion share glances and brief comments, a couple of times smiles and laughs. A fragile truce? A frail alliance in humanity? A glimmer of interpersonal integrity against staggering odds? Do I project, as if navigating still a house of mirrors, too much of my 40-something outlook onto this younger generation? Are my White students "colorblind" in some way more informed than I presume? Will my Black students ever trust me for bringing race matters up in class, risking the blowback of resentful Whites on the one hand, Latinos on the other hand wondering whenever "brown" will be relevant? Meanwhile and increasingly, Asian (American mostly, but increasingly Chinese national) students mostly stare blankly ahead; mute vigils of this never-ending saga, wary of stereotypes littered everywhere. This is the melodrama of the American classroom across our land, which I face like an ersatz Juror 8, parading around the room challenging holdout students with something like, "Isn't it *possible* that the brutal illusion of race is with us still?" Yes, it's possible that objects in the mirror are larger than they appear. It's possible. But is that the best we can do? Weren't we supposed to do this a long time ago? Is that all there is to learn? *The more we run from it, the more we run into it. It's an age old story.*

POSTSCRIPT

Crater Lake, in Oregon, features water clear enough to see 150 feet deep. The lake was formed from a series of massive explosions essentially blowing what was an 11,000 foot mountain nearly to its base. The lake is aptly named for that matter, but unlike most craters, it cradles the bluest of azure blue I've ever seen. The water supplied to the lake is entirely rainfall and snow runoff along rock scree. Because there is no loam along the banks, there is virtually no siltation in the water. The lake's clarity is not rated among the Wonders of the World, but it should be. I first saw this lake up close when I was sixteen. With our mother and one of our German cousins, my twin brother and I drove my sister to start classes at the San Francisco Conservatory of Music. We stopped off at the lake and, defying local convention that nobody dares swim in the lake because it's too cold, scurried to the water's edge across loose scree and plunged in from a rock face overhang. I remember eyeing the rock face as it descended ever deeper into the abyss. This experience, like so many I had growing up, shaped in me what similar experiences have shaped for White post-Baby Boomers everywhere, which would give rise to the second wave environmental movement for natural areas conservation over the last 30 years.

Very few Black people have visited Crater Lake, much less swum in it. Most Black people in this country grow up like Jackie and her family under circumstances removed from the kind of Elysian experiences I was so privileged to have. Now every living system on this planet is in decline because of the conspicuous consumption of the privileged like me among us. Meanwhile, the environmental movement has been remarkably slow to make the link between poverty, race, and environmental degradation. Everywhere Whites have sunk deep taproot, like English Ivy, invading every nook and cranny worth invading on this continent. Everywhere people of color have been denied sinking those taproots. Everywhere we take our privileges with us, for us: Whites have affiliated living well with living apart, hobbling urban tax bases that could have otherwise sustained truly beautiful places and sustaining bioregions, nourished by the rich cultural and intellectual heritage that peoples of color endow to this country. Meanwhile, good White liberals believe in their various causes. But they don't see what their taproots have done. How to unhook from a taproot is no straightforward matter. What will a jury of our future peers have to say about our culpability?

REFERENCES

Blackman, H. (1978). *Regents of Univ. of Cal. v. Bakke*, 438 U.S. 265, 407.
Marsalis, W. (2000). Interview. In K. Burns & L. Novick (Producers), *Jazz: A film by Ken Burns,* Episode One. New York: Florentine Films.

ROSA MAZURETT-BOYLE & RENÉ ANTROP-GONZÁLEZ

8. OUR JOURNEYS AS LATIN@ EDUCATORS AND THE PERPETUAL STRUGGLE TO UNHOOK FROM WHITENESS

A central perspective that weaves the chapters of this book is that our work as nondominant individuals does not aim to move us closer to the normative center of White society. Instead, we seek to honor and uphold our differences, whatever they may be, as they make us strong. In this chapter, we examine Resistance Capital (Yosso, 2006) as a way to broaden the conceptualization of normalcy, as formulated in Whiteness, and to advantage all the elements that influence our own Latin@ness. Here we seek to examine the one question: How do we as hybrid U.S. Latin@s, operating within Whiteness, simultaneously resist and capitalize on our Latin@ness to succeed in our professional and personal lives?

We begin by offering our definitions for two terms: Latin@ness and Resistance. Then we turn to scholarly research to situate succinctly our own definitions within the context of existing academic conversation around Latin@s and resistance and, in this way, give way to our epistemological stance on "resistance as capital" (Yosso, 2005). Subsequently we describe our methodological strategies and present *testimonios* as the way to document and later analyze our positionality as nondominant individuals and scholars. Lastly, we provide both a discussion and conclusion.

Agreeing to define ourselves through the term Latin@ness was easy. In this chapter, the letters and arroba symbol in the word Latin@ness afford us a space to examine the complexity of constructing our identities as U.S. Latin@s within a larger framework that speaks to the uses of the pan-ethnic labels Hispanic/Latino.[1] Inherently using Latin@ or Hispanic is problematic because independently these terms *Other* and simultaneously unite us in disrupting the oppression caused by not unhooking from Whiteness. Throughout this chapter our discussion of ethnic/race, gender, social, and transnational experiences fall within the overarching category of identity. Although we will specifically define our experiences in set categories such as female-male, mother-father, teacher-professor, Chilean-Puerto Rican both of French-Spaniard and indigenous descents, bilingual, (im)migrant, transnational, and African, as U.S. raised individuals, we also use the term Latin@ness to bridge our individual experiences and dualities to diverse Latin@ communities. Similarly, our definition of resistance includes opposition, preservation/adaptation, and healing. Opposition grows from one's own raising of political consciousness or

C. Hayes and N.D. Hartlep (Eds.), Unhooking from Whiteness:
The Key to Dismantling Racism in the United States, 103–121.
© *2013 Sense Publishers. All Rights Reserved.*

conscientization (Freire, 1990) around the erosive effect institutional models and modes of operation have on nondominant beliefs, values, practices, and languages. In resisting, as acts, we preserve and adjust our ways of knowing to the worlds that we live in. Resistance becomes capital we use to fight efforts to sterilize our identities, and it serves to battle emotional and other forms of aggressions (Yosso, Smith, Ceja, & Solórzano, 2009). Resistance restores power to our voices enabling us to produce change, and, in acting on our power, we embark in healing as we unhook from the narrow and oppressive practices of Whiteness. The process of resistance makes us whole by allowing us to take culturally cohesive stands and to reclaim self-respect from unremitting historically instituted injustices.

BACKGROUND

It is important to indicate that our use of Latin@ness stipulates that this term is a powerful concept in the formation of identity and is grounded in academic literature. From the fields of Latino Studies, Chicano Studies, and Education a significant body of literature examines the broad and deeply complex issues in defining the U.S. Latin@ experience in general and in education specifically. Much scholarship in these fields attempts to peel back centuries of historic, social, economic, and political factors that shape the lives and address the challenges of forming U.S. Latin@ identities (Flores, 1993; González, 2011; Hurtado & Gurin, 2004; San Miguel, 2011; Springer, 2009; Urrieta, 2009; Valdés, Gonzáles, López García & Márquez, 2003). Similarly, multicultural and critical scholars working in the fields of second language education and linguistics address the question of the Latin@ experience by examining second language acquisition and heritage/cultural maintenance. In general, we find research on teaching practices and goals that promote second language learning (Lucas, 2011; Luria, Seymour, & Smoke, 2006) while others address sociopolitical issues that arise from having individuals learn the dominant language at the expense of the nondominant language. Spanish becomes subjugated to majority language policies, depriving Latin@ students opportunities to learn use, and maintain their home language and culture in schools (Crawford, 1992; Reagan, 2009; Spring, 2009). In studying language from a sociocultural lens, language becomes a tool in the formulation, mediation, and alteration of personal and group experiences as well as a tool of power and resistance (Crawford & Krashen, 2007; Kubota & Lin, 2009; Pennycook, 2010). In addition, language learning research converges on the interconnections of personal and group experiences and its impact on identity provides insights on issues concerning nondominant language maintenance and attrition, second language prestige, linguistic variations among Latin@ groups and among cohort of immigrant groups, as well as documenting European languages dominance on indigenous languages and cultures (Caminero-Santangelo, 2007; Lantolf & Sunderman, 2001; Santa Ana, 2004; Valdés, 2001; Valdés, Fishman, Chávez, & Pérez, 2008; Zentella,1997; 2005).

A broad range of social science and educational research engaged in analyzing the Latin@ experience considers other factors such as ethnicity, race, gender, age, religion, (im)migration stages, and transnational dimensions in identity formation, educational pipeline, and engagement of multi-lingual/multi-cultural realities in daily experiences (Amaro & Zambran 2000; Antrop-González, Vélez, & Garrett, 2005; Delgado Bernal, Elenes, Godinez, & Villenas, 2006; Fergus, 2009; Gándara & Contreras, 2010; Martín Alcoff, 2006; Nieto, 2002; Ochoa, 2007; Sanchez & Machado-Casas, 2009; Tellez, 2004; Villenas, 2009). In the same manner, the study of Latin@ experiences is related to research on issues of social and economic inequality, power, access, and resistance lived by multi-generational Latin@ individuals and groups. Here research centers on the influence of policies, the politics of knowledge and pedagogy, and academic achievement in the pipeline (Irizarry & Donaldson, 2012; Kiyama, 2010; Murillo, Villenas, Galván, Sánchez Muñoz, Martínez, & Machado-Casas, 2010; Spring, 2008; Suárez-Orozco & Páez, 2009; Valenzuela, 1999).

In this chapter, the term Latin@ness allow us to bring into focus slices of our lives as *testimonios* (Murillo et al., 2010), substantiating reoccurring themes in the scholarship, and to ground our Latin@ness in the fluidity of our lived experiences, skills, and knowledge. Building on existing literature, we convey how our historically accumulated experiences guide our trajectory towards unhooking from Whiteness. Over time and through deep and sincere analysis of our own autobiographical data, we take on our own research questions: How do we construct hybrid identities as U.S. Latin@s operating within Whiteness, in luminal spaces that simultaneously resist assimilative practices and help us capitalize on our Latin@ness to succeed in our professional and personal lives?

THEORETICAL FRAMEWORK: RESISTANT CAPITAL

This chapter draws on Yosso's (2006) concept of Resistance Capital within her model of Community Cultural Wealth, which brings into play two major theoretical frameworks: Critical Race Theory (CRT) and social and cultural capital. Whereas the concept of resistance is vigorously supported in CRT scholarship (Bonilla-Silva, 2009), the conceptualization of nondominant forms of social and cultural capital continues to be a contested topic (Lubienski, 2003; Oughton, 2010; Ríos-Aguilar, Kiyama, Gravitt, & Moll, 2011; Yosso, 2005; 2006). In this chapter, we put forth that the concept of resistance is relevant in expanding definitions of Latin@ness, and we discuss how it conflicts with what counts as normal behaviors, beliefs, attitudes, values, and practices of Whiteness. Resistance is an important component of cultural wealth that allows us to begin the healing process from historic and systemic oppression and dehumanization. As such, everyday forms of resistance become valuable tools in the struggle towards the validation of the cultural expertise and social connections we draw on to define Latin@ness and in our professional and personal lives to unhooking from Whiteness.

Resistance capital is grounded in the work of Bourdieu (1986). In general, both social and cultural capital can be reduced to power, which inherently seeks to preserve and reproduce pre-existing inequalities and competencies that ensure social or cultural advancement of the dominant society (Bourdieu, 2003; Olneck, 2000; Stampnitzky, 2006). Typically, social capital is defined as accumulated or potential resources and relations associated with membership in a social group (Olneck, 2000). More specifically, Portes (1998, 2000) offers that social capital functions as "a source of social control, a source of family-mediated benefits, and a source of resources mediated by nonfamily networks" (2000, p. 2) and as such contributes to social reproduction of attributes of the dominant group (Monkman, Ronald, & Théramène, 2005). In turn, cultural capital represents skills and accumulated knowledge inherited or possessed by groups of society. Following this line of thinking, the unequal participation of nondominant groups in positions of power situates their practices, skills, and ways of knowing as abnormal reducing opportunities for nondominant individuals or groups to gain access to social and economic benefits (Bourdieu & Passeron, 1970; Foucault, 1979/1984; Monkman, Ronald, & Théramène, 2005). Thus, the notion of normality gives way to common misconceptions, for instance that nondominant children begin schooling at a disadvantage from their White peers and over time cannot succeed (De Gaetano, 2007). These false assertions often serve to justify poor representation of nondominant groups in positions of power in institutions, such as schools and universities, without acutely examining the deep structures of schooling and the broad connections to other social organizations (Mulkey, 1993; Tyke, 2000).

Critics of Auto-Ethnographic Academic Research

As critical reflexive practitioners, researchers, and educators, our work—and, at times, even our presence—politicizes the conditions of nondominant students and educators. However, it is important to note the existence of an ongoing criticism of auto-ethnographic research, which has been described as too narrow or too specific to represent the Latin@ experience or be meaningful to mainstream research (Delamont, 2009; Ngunjiri, Hernandez, & Chang, 2010; Yosso, 2005). Hughes, Pennington, and Makris (2012) offer that auto-ethnographic research is often disregarded as valid and reproducible research. Consequently, scholars conducting auto-ethnographic research are penalized when coming up for academic promotions and tenure (Ladson-Billings, 2005). We considered these criticisms when writing this chapter as we set out to expound on our experiences as a way to articulate ways in which our lived experiences become resources to battle in daily struggles to unhook from Whiteness and systemic dehumanization.

However, in the context of this chapter, our intent is neither to become the voice of U.S. Latin@s nor to provide a how-to guide for deciphering the U.S. Latin@ experience. According to Delgado Bernal (2008) and Pérez Huber (2009), *testimonios*, as counterstories, are tools that reveal visible and invisible ways

Eurocentric, racist, classist, male dominate, and heteronormative epistemologies dehumanize nondominant individuals or groups by maintaining institutional, educational, economic, and racist inequalities in our society. The systematic and ethical analysis of our auto-ethnographies and *testimonios* puts us in dialogue with multiple ideologies, epistemologies, and educational practices in and out of the White normalized research realms. The use of *testimonio* also affords us the opportunity to participate in the academic dialogue involving the validity of individuals' everyday experiences to answer the question: How do we construct hybrid identities as U.S. Latin@s operating within Whiteness in liminal positions that simultaneously resist assimilative practices and help us capitalize on our Latin@ness to succeed in our professional and personal lives? At the same time, we aspire to highlight the dearth of educational inquiries voicing the resistance wealth of multi-gender, multi-ethnic, multi-lingual, and transnational educators working in kindergarten-through-16 settings through our respective positions as a classroom teacher and a teacher educator. Our work has a serious political goal, which is to challenge research agendas defined by White institutions that exclude authentic Latin@ voices. We aim to combine theory and praxis to challenge Whiteness, to inculcate consciousness of the abundance of nondominant cultural capital in our students, and to move teaching and education towards social justice.

Yosso's community cultural wealth model delineates narratives that account for a broader explanation of what counts as cultural capital. In her 2005 germinal work "Whose Culture Has Capital?", Yosso questions paradigms in academic research and educational practices that serve to oppress and dismiss nondominant groups' "lived experiences and histories" (p. 71). These paradigms are problematic, since they marginalize nondominant beliefs, values, and social practices. Furthermore, Yosso's definition of culture reaffirms the stance that culture is not monolithic and does not have fixed characteristics, although commonalities surface among groups that serve to distinguish collective diversity (González, 2005; Rogoff, 2003). As it applies to education, the position of the community cultural wealth model centers around theories of cultural and social capital that "have been used to assert that some communities are culturally wealthy while others are culturally poor," (Yosso, 2005, p. 76) perpetuating deficit views about nondominant individuals and communities. Consequently, the notion of community cultural wealth as capital proposes that within the hybridity of nondominant groups there are specific elements that support individual differences and give a voice to honor and build on differences.

The community cultural wealth model validates the use of auto-ethnographic counterstories and *testimonios* as methodology. Critical scholars have long argued that nondominant individuals and their lived experiences are excluded from dominant research, which simultaneously silences and marginalizes nondominant ways of knowing (Ladson-Billings & Tate, 1995; Solórzano & Delgado Bernal, 2001; Yosso, 2006). This systemic silencing and exclusion undoubtedly influences research agendas and the definitions of what constitutes social and cultural capital within and for Latin@ communities. Simultaneously, the lack of culturally responsive research agendas negates the possibility of demystifying definitions of what constitutes social and cultural capital to nondominant individuals and their group affiliations. In other words, the premium placed on social connections, social mobility, linguistic and cultural competencies, competition, and economic power for two Latin@s is different from those of a middle-class White educator.

Therefore, counterstories from nondominant perspectives are narratives excluded from academic research agendas (Ladson-Billings, 2005). By using them here, our *testimonios* become not only instruments of resistance against oppressive research agendas driven by White institutions but also valuable research material for other nondominant scholars, because we faithfully narrate systemic oppression (Yosso, 2006) and validate elements that make up a notion of Latin@ cultural wealth.

Our personal narratives aim to recognize our experiences not as tales of the marginalized but, instead, as valuable social and cultural capital resources others can use towards ending racism. In saying this, we recognize that our epistemology is consistent with CRT scholarship that articulates ways in which nondominant groups build on historical knowledge and lived experiences to resist social, political, economic, gender, religious, and linguistic forms of oppression, systemic inequality, and assimilation. Likewise, Yosso (2006) asserts that collections of personal and social experiences anchor valuable forms of capital including aspirational, familial, social, navigational, linguistic, and resistant to Latin@ communities across the U.S., cultivating and generating richly complex interpretations of community cultural wealth. In other words, as a model, community cultural wealth acknowledges that Latin@s as members of U.S. nondominant groups possess unique forms of Latin@ ness that help us maneuver our lives away from oppression and towards emancipation within subaltern (Ladson-Billings, 2005) spaces.

Therefore, the individual construction of our Latin@ness grounded in historical and personal perspectives documents ways we strategize unhooking from Whiteness. Our goal is not to move towards Whiteness; instead, it is to broaden the circle of "normalcy" and perspectives inherent in Whiteness (Delgado & Stefancic, 2001; Harris, 1993). We contend that through the conscious and unconscious process of unhooking from Whiteness, as a form of resistance, we create unique forms of capital that in turn enrich our lives, the lives of our families, and the work we do as scholars and practitioners. In the following section, we describe the methods we used to write this chapter.

METHODS

Research Design, Data, and Analysis

Data collected for this chapter include auto-ethnographic biographies, a series of *testimonios* reporting and reflection on specific events, researchers' notes, and memos. During the process of data collection and analysis, we scheduled face-to-face meetings to clarify our positions, definitions, and interpretations of the data. Independently, we kept field notes of the process and meetings that later formed part of the larger text data. The text data was continuously examined for emerging themes and categories were reorganized. During the multiple data analysis stages, we looked for initial and conceptual themes to construct a larger picture of ways we strategized our unhooking from Whiteness and its implications for our work as Latin@ educators. The *testimonios* and author field notes were carefully analyzed to understand how we interpret our multi-generational lived and professional experiences in the context of Latin@ness and resistance. Our analytic lens, as outsiders, helped us to consider themes, relationships, and other ways we construct normalcy outside the realms of Whiteness.

Data and Data Collection

A few years back, René and I met while presenting on a conference panel pertaining to reconceptualizations of funds of knowledge (Moll, Amanti, Neff, & González, 1995). Later we began collaborating on a project framed by *testimonio* scholarship focusing on the mentoring relationship between a Latin@ teacher educator and a Latina teacher completing a doctoral program. Although we live in different parts of the country, drawing on our professional and personal interests has become a form of social capital. For this particular project, we agreed to answer an in-depth questionnaire to construct autobiographies. The interview protocol covered childhood and present families, social networks, education histories and opportunities, socioeconomic status, professional experiences, interpretations of Latin@ness, and resistance.

ROSA'S TESTIMONIO

I was born in Chile the year Paolo Freire was released from prison. Freire moved to Chile joining likeminded individuals working towards educational, social, political, and economic reform. I provide this historical detail to help you visualize the groundbreaking effort undertaken by the Chilean government, citizens, and international organizations to bring about sweeping social, political, economic, and educational reform, and its lasting influence on my worldviews about oppression and dehumanization, which guide my work towards unhooking from Whiteness. Between 1964 and 1973, two Chilean presidents supported and actively promoted political, economic, and social institutional changes to strengthen economic balance and guarantee democratic regulations for all Chileans (Milos, 2004). During this decade, social justice and equity framed institutional reform avoiding previous perceptions that branded social justice as charity for the poor. For instance, Chilean officials with the help of world organizations sought equitable redistribution of economic assets through a series of legislative measures that transformed land laborers into landowners, altering the power structures that frame social class. Following the same line of socio-economic reform, the government expropriated copper mines from international hands, securing financial gains for Chileans (Cox, Munro-Faure, Mathieu, Herrera, Palmer, et al, 2003).

The social revolution also extended to the educational system. By the time I entered kindergarten, universities and government had invested heavily in teacher preparation, innovative pedagogies, and curriculum development aiming to promote critical pedagogy, social justice, and humanization (Milos, 2004). Although I was young, I recognized that I was part of an intellectual revolution, and my academic instruction was framed by what I recognize now as anti-oppressive pedagogy (Freire, 1990). After the political coup of 1973, the educational revolution came to a halt. Unfortunately, those in power used oppressive and violent tactics to revert civil, political, educational, and economic freedoms. During this time, although I was just a child, I knew that friends and family feared for their lives. More and more people were disappearing. Families desperately and secretly sought the help of humanitarian organizations to locate loved ones. Fear permeated every aspect of our lives. Mami told us kids to trust nobody; neighbors were turning against neighbors, and the slightest slip of the tongue could lead to loved ones to appearing on the *desaparecidos* list [the disappeared/the missing].

My childhood was full of unexpected and radical changes. When I was three years old, my father died suddenly, and with his death our social and economic status crashed. We moved houses, my siblings attended new schools, and eventually our mother had to go to work to support herself and five kids. Soon after the military coup, we attended a Catholic school, which provided some stability as they continued to embrace, in secret, the familiar social justice paradigms of my earlier schooling experiences. Then, in the mid-1970s, my family left Chile and settled in the United States. Immigrating to the U.S. was indeed an ironic twist of fate considering the important role U.S. international policies played in the overthrow of a democratically elected government and its support for the military regime. Strangely enough, my family did not harvest resentment against the United States. Instead, we felt grateful to escape death and persecution. Once in the U.S., Mami put in long hours at the factory, and within a few years of skillful financial planning, she was able to buy a modest house. Her brick and mortar dream, like for countless other immigrants, meant security and stability for her children.

As long as I remember, Mami put our education first, and afterward, when I returned to school for my doctoral degree, she put my family first. Her generosity helped me reach my educational goals and validated her lifelong commitment to education and family. For her, education is a basic need; she insists that *educación* [education] is the most important bequest parents leave children. Naturally, she defines education in two ways. The first definition refers to the acquisition of academic knowledge and skills, as well as the achievement of milestones from kindergarten to college that allows individuals to attain personal, professional, and financial success. The second definition alludes to teaching children skill sets, beliefs, values, and practices that successfully merge what children learn in households with the socially accepted practices of other networks and communities.

In the U.S., I attended the urban school district where I now teach. During my middle and high school years, few teachers acknowledged Mami's strength of character, hard work, financial expertise, definitions of *educación*, and her resourcefulness as social and cultural wealth (Yosso, 2006). Instead, my Latin@ness was constructed as "at risk" (Gardner, 1983). It is true that I grew up economically poor and, by default, our "lack" of economic capital position put us in tension with White middle class attitudes. At that time, I did not know I was "at risk;" I only knew that Mami never saw high school graduation as the final goal for our academic careers. Instead, she expected that her children would attend college or learn a trade. All five of us graduated from high school, and four of us attended college. Sadly, our academic success, strong familial ties, Spanish language maintenance, English language acquisition, preservation of cultural values, beliefs and practices, and personal ambitions were not recognized as cultural capital in school.

At 16, I started my college career. I envisioned college students coming together to challenge the *status quo* and mold new realities that promoted social justice and equality. As an undergraduate, I came face-to-face with middle-class ways of seeing the world. I spent two years trying to fit in socially, toiled to prove myself academically while questioning my cultural and ethnic membership. Questions about my membership and belonging became salient, as I was one of a handful Spanish-speaking Latin@s attending that well-known liberal arts college in the state. I altered my physical appearance, speech, and attitudes to blend in with the majority of White middle-class students. My efforts to blend and pass for a dominant individual proved fruitless. For instance, I made an appointment with a humanities professor, because I was struggling to construct a historically "correct" narrative for a paper. He advised me to "never speak Spanish again" if I wanted to improve my English and understand Western culture. At the same time, he insinuated that a pretty girl like me could always find ways to get a better grade in his course. The discourse endorsing English and dominant culture as superior to my home language made me furious, and his advances made me feel self-conscious, disempowered, lonely, and dirty. Eventually I graduated with two degrees and moved to Europe. I eventually returned to the United States and returned to school for my Masters degree in bilingual education.

Professional Experience

My first teaching jobs were in suburban high schools, because they offered a family friendly schedule that benefited my own children. As a native Spanish speaker, I often taught advanced level courses. However, my linguistic skills, international teaching experience, or graduate degree did not exempt me from the distrust of parents and students. While working in a school district adjacent to the inner city, the administrator of the high school asked me to send letters to my students' parents detailing my professional experience and educational background, because parents complained about my use of Spanish, particularly in the instructional materials of the course. Although other White teachers used the materials and curriculum, I was the only one who had to justify its use in my courses. The request was unwelcomed and clearly discriminatory; however, Cobas and Feagin (2008) document other cases where nondominant educators' skills and professional qualifications regularly fall under the suspicion and fear of suburban parents.

Once our own children started school, I purposefully sought a full-time position in the urban school district I attended as a high school student. For ten years, I taught in an elementary school experiencing White flight. By the tenth year, nondominant students made up the student body. However, the Latin@ teacher workforce in the school and throughout the school district remained below the national average of 7 percent (Mancuso, 2010; NCES, 2009). As the only Latina teacher in that urban school, as a one-person department, and as one of three elementary Spanish language teachers in the entire county, I felt isolated and ill prepared for the job (Irizarry & Donaldson, 2012). As time passed, I noticed that the needs of my student population were changing; however, the administrative policies and curriculum I had to implement in the classroom were designed for White middle-class students. My frustration and desire to improve students' academic success, in meaningful ways, led me to pursue a doctorate program. My initial goal was to become a better teacher, particularly for my Spanish heritage language learners. I wanted to find ways to facilitate a shift in paradigm from resisting Spanish and Latin@ cultures to embracing cultures and historically accumulated funds of knowledge (González, Moll, & Amanti, 2005). By that time, I developed the pragmatic belief that schooling practices which underpin Latin@ culture and language as *foreign* harm Latin@ students at the level of the soul.

The systemic oppression and racism experienced in educational settings harm the soul of nondominant individuals, and the harmful effects are not exclusive to school age children. Sadly, my professional preparation to become a teacher left out the work of Latin@ scholars. During my doctoral coursework, I discovered that a handful of Latin@ researchers were finding ways to participate in the academic dialogue that positions cultural and social knowledge developed in Latin@ homes and communities as meaningful and worthy of research. The epistemological stands of nondominant researchers, as well as the ways they understood their roles as researchers, spoke to me about my own experiences through a lens that I recognized as my own. Nevertheless, we still have a long way to go in being included in academic dialogue or in the curriculum of teacher preparation programs. Certainly, nondominant scholars have pursued lines of inquiry that have meaningfully affected the scholarship of world language education, Second Language Acquisition (SLA), and funds of knowledge. Furthermore, academic research agendas concerned with nondominant students serve to inform my own research as a teacher-researcher and the research I conduct with other practitioners in my school district.

Today I teach in a high school, and my students often ask, "If you are a doctor, why are you here?" After many conversations with students, parents, and peers, I realize that I am here to support students in finding ways to honor and respect their own ways of knowing within a hostile educational system. Looking back on my historically accumulated experiences as an immigrant, and with ongoing reflection on my funds of knowledge, definitions of education, and experiences as a Latin@ student, teacher, and mother, I view my day-to-day work as a form of resistance capital. Individuals like me seek to understand students' funds of knowledge and draw on them to drive instruction. I believe I have the power to help students and ourselves to stay on the path towards unhooking from Whiteness and healing from the effects of racism.

As a high school classroom teacher, I take a day-by-day approach to disrupting White dominance through resistance. In my role as a teacher in the process of Unhooking from Whiteness, I promote positive cultural identity while advancing Spanish language learning. As a researcher, I reflect on my position to identify capital wealth and funds of knowledge to continue my journey of transgression across curriculum, teaching, and learning. So if I am asked, "Why are you here?", I simply reply that I am here to humanize the educational experience for all of us.

RENÉ'S TESTIMONIO

My New England Ricaness: My Early Years

I am of two distinct socio-political worlds. I am of the colonizer and the colonized. I am a DiaspoRican bilingual and bicultural border crosser. I am a Puerto Rican who resides in the United States. I am a colonized subject who once was and still is dehumanized. I was, am, and will constantly be born of Operations Bootstrap and Serenity. In 1968, my first-generation United States father was sent to Juana Díaz, Puerto Rico from Rhode Island to work at the General Electric (GE) facility in *La Ciudad de Los Tres Reyes*. As a young supervisor, he was trained in the problematic arts of modeling capitalism and progress to Puerto Ricans. It was during his two years at GE that he met my mother, who was a secretary there. Their courtship was brief, as they married in 1969. By this time, GE had summoned him back to his native Rhode Island to continue his work with the company. In fact, to this day, he still recounts how some of his colleagues had half-jokingly admonished him for having "married one of the Puerto Rican locals" while on the Island. On the other hand, my mother had never been to the United States and was often left wondering why she had left her family only to find herself in the God-forsaken, long winters of New England.

By the time I was born in 1970, my mother had become depressed due to the cold weather, a lack of familial support, and the general lack of other Puerto Ricans in the Ocean State. Moreover, the prospects of raising a growing family compelled my father to work extremely long hours in order to obtain additional financial security. Consequently, my mother requested that my father send for my grandmother in order to ease her feelings of loneliness. My grandmother, as a result, would spend considerable time with my mother and me. Thus, from a very early age, I would hear the sounds of Spanish and smell the sweet aromas of *arroz, habichuelas, y sofrito*. Eventually, my father would tire of working long hours in both Rhode Island and "Taxachusetts", because he felt his paychecks were getting smaller due to high taxes in those states. In 1976 (I was eight), my father was offered a job with another defense contractor known as Martin Marietta (now Lockheed Martin), which is located in Orlando, Florida. My father was ecstatic, because he would not have to pay local or state income taxes thanks to Florida's tourist industry, which supposedly subsidizes a majority of social services. I still remember the three-day trip from Massachusetts to Florida with my parents, two younger sisters, my grandmother Mamá Tita, and my uncle Tío Carlos. Finally we arrived to our brand new home in the Gatlin Heights neighborhood. We would end up being the only Puerto Ricans on the block there, however, as *Boricuas* had not quite yet discovered the Sunshine State.

Growing up Orlando Rican

Upon starting the second grade at Michael McCoy Elementary School in Orlando, I distinctly remember being a Puerto Rican in a sea of Whiteness. I do not remember any of my teachers making a conscious effort to make curriculum culturally and/ or linguistically relevant for me. Consequently, I began to resist and act out my frustrations. Hence, many of my teachers began to label me as a "problem child" and as a "discipline case." This unfortunate labeling led to teachers notifying my mother of the fact that I was hard to deal with at school. My mother therefore found herself being my advocate. My mother's new role of advocate in this Orlando public school was a daunting one for her. She felt that she was not afforded the same level of respect as other parents/caregivers because of her strong presence as a woman of color and her Puerto Rican Spanish accent, and she also felt many teachers spoke down to her and thought of her as being less intelligent because of her ethnicity. Indeed, unlike many of the schools in Orlando today, there were no bilingual teachers and/or other Latina/o staff members who could have served as entry points to schools that were largely White. Several years of these culturally and linguistically narrow practices went on until, at the beginning of my sixth grade year, I began to notice that several Puerto Rican students were class peers of mine for the first time. As a result, the parents of these students began to seek my mother out since they had heard of her advocacy role within the school.

With this new influx of Puerto Rican migrants to Orlando, I began to witness several changes in Orlando. By the time I reached high school in 1985, one of the most important changes included the establishment of a Puerto Rican business community, which was located on State Road 436 about 15 miles north of the Orlando International Airport. It was in this business district that I could have a plate of *arroz con habichuelas* or an *alcapurria* with a *jugo de tamarindo*. With this substantial arrival of *Boricuas* to Orlando, I finally felt like I belonged in this growing urban center. In fact, I remember having great fun bagging groceries and stocking shelves at the Publix near where I lived, because I was able to converse in Spanish with many of our Puerto Rican customers. However, it was also by speaking Spanish at my job that I quickly learned how political language could be, as the monolingual English speakers around me often exchanged unfriendly glances in my direction. Rather than switch back to English, I felt I had no choice but to respond with a political message of linguistic resistance of my very own—I would just continue to speak Spanish with my Puerto Rican customers.

By 1990, when I was in my second year in college, Orlando had definitely become a major center of Puerto Rican migration. I remember the frequent display of Puerto Rican flags, the sounds of *salsa* and *merengue*, the sight of low riders with Puerto Rican flags on rearview mirrors, and outdoor festivals celebrating Puerto Rican music and culture. In fact, it was at this particular time in my life that I thought another way to reconnect with my Puerto Ricaness was to major in Spanish and increase my travels to see my family in Puerto Rico. Eventually, in 1993, I earned my undergraduate degree in Spanish from the University of Central Florida. However, I still found myself bagging groceries at the same Publix two months after graduation, which made my decision as to what to do next in my life that much easier. I decided to fulfill my dream of moving to Puerto Rico. I taught English in Juana Díaz, pursued graduate studies in Ponce, and spent a total of five years on the Island. More importantly, I met my partner. Wanda and I met during a political rally, fell in love, and got married—we did all these things in a period of six months. Eventually, our two beautiful daughters were born in Ponce. In 1998, we left Puerto Rico, because I was offered a doctoral fellowship to pursue studies in curriculum and instruction with an emphasis in bilingual education at The Pennsylvania State University.

Currently, we reside in Milwaukee, Wisconsin with the addition of our son, François. Although I have not lived in Orlando since 1993, I go back on an occasional basis to visit my parents. Moreover, I am now involved in a research project, which examines the experiences of Puerto Rican high school youth in Central Florida high schools. I am more than convinced that my teaching, research, and service have been greatly impacted by my own negative schooling experiences as an Orlando Rican youth. Consequently, I am determined to make further sense of the schooling experiences of Puerto Rican youth and to work with teachers who strive to serve them precisely because much research suggests that the educational attainment of these youth still lags far behind their White peers. In essence, then, I feel like I have returned home in a roundabout way.

What Does Puerto Rican Orlando Look Like Now?

The Puerto Rican Orlando I knew growing up continues to grow. For instance, according to the recent scholarly work of Jorge Duany and Félix Matos-Rodríguez (2006), Orlando is the "fourth largest metropolitan area for Puerto Ricans in the United States, after New York City, Philadelphia, and Chicago" (p. 3). Moreover, while the high school attainment rates among Puerto Ricans are higher in Central Florida due to higher English proficiency rates (Duany & Matos-Rodríguez, 2006), most Latin@/Puerto Rican high school students "perform below statewide averages in 10th grade Reading and Math FCAT examinations" (De Jesús & Vazquez, 2007; p. 3). The FCAT exam is the high-stakes high school exit exam required of all youth who aspire to obtain a regular high school diploma. Thus, it is imperative that policy makers and educators alike strive to construct policies that will enable Puerto Ricans who reside in Orlando to increase their life chances and structures of opportunity. In many ways, then, the Orlando I grew up in is still trying to make sense of its newest (im)migrants.

Although I have made Milwaukee my home, I still tell people that I grew up an Orlando Rican. However, I still think about the extent to which my identity is once again in flux. I can also consider myself a Milwaukee Rican. Our children could also consider themselves Milwaukee Ricans. Will Wanda consider herself one day to be a DiaspoRican although she was born and raised on the Island? Who gets to construct Puerto Rican identity and at whose expense? Finally, while I identify as Puerto Rican, I cannot simply ignore race and phenotype and the privileges or lack thereof that one garners from such social constructions and their society-ascribed meanings. As a light skinned, heterosexual, bilingual/bicultural, middle class scholar, and able-bodied DiaspoRican, I am afforded the privilege of crossing a multiplicity of racial/ethnic and linguistic borders. Consequently, some of the people I engage with view me as being "one of them" and use this assumption to verbally express their racist, classist, homophobic, and sexist views. Therefore, I work to interrupt those conversations, which often takes some by surprise. I read their facial expressions as asking, "Are you not White?" I respond, "I am Puerto Rican, and I strive to work in solidarity with people of color and other marginalized groups." Hence, these statements serve as my way of unhooking myself from Whiteness. These are questions and moments of racial interruption I still ask and engage in, as I continue to think about my journey to construct and claim my Orlando Rican identity—to claim my OtheRicaness and unhook from Whiteness.

DISCUSSION AND CONCLUSION

The original question we posed to ourselves as we embarked in the process of self-analysis and the study of our professional experiences was how do we, as hybrid U.S. Latin@s operating within Whiteness, simultaneously resist and capitalize on our Latin@ness to succeed in our professional and personal lives. Two central findings emerged from the data analysis. One addresses the issue of agency, and the other refers to professional training. In the following section, we discuss these two issues.

Agency: ¿Somos víctimas? [Are We Victims?]

During our discussions, the notion of victimization emerged in intricate ways. Our *testimonios* and our work as scholars point out that nondominant individuals and groups are victimized by systematic and unwavering political, economic, and social stratagems to strip nondominant culture and languages from immigrants. However, viewing oneself as a victim may appear incongruent with the notion of Resistance Capital. Our definition of resistance specifies that resistance becomes capital when we are able to identify the forces exerting oppression. Big or small acts of opposition give us the power to reclaim what we value, and help us to make our soul whole once again.

In our life histories, both René and I speak of large and small systematic efforts of policies, social canon, and economic distribution of wealth that aimed to eradicate our Latin@ness. Throughout our historical accounts, we share multiple strategies we learned to identify covert and overt oppressive forces. Moreover, we note our use of collective knowledge to resist hegemony, and chronicle instances when we triumph over oppressive practices. In some instances, we passed for White—we recognized the oppressive practices, ignored them, and went on—while at other junctures, we channeled our energy to protest against injustices and to share our knowledge with friends, families, and students-peers on how to resist. These collections of lived experiences contribute to the formation of our Latin@ness and to capitalization from resistance.

Issues of Resistance through Latin@ Teacher Voices

Both of our narratives speak to the absence of culturally relevant curriculum. Although staffing schools with nondominant educators often emerges as a critical concern to educators, the reality is that 83% of the teaching workforce continues to be White and female (NCES, 2009). Although current population trends project steady increases in Latin@ student populations through 2020 (NCES, 2011), Rosa's perspectives, experiences, and voice as a Latina teacher infrequently appears in scholarship. While we expect that the nondominant student population will be the majority by midcentury, the national teacher workforce in kindergarten through 12th grade only includes 6.7% Latin@ educators (NCES, 2011b). Unfortunately, these low numbers also indicate that lived experiences and voices of Latin@ educators will continue to be absent from White dominated institutions. Nondominant teachers will continue to participate in research designed for and primarily by White academics informing research agendas favored by White institutions (Kubota & Lin, 2009; Ladson Billings, 2005; Yosso, 2006). For nondominant teachers like Rosa, unhooking from Whiteness (dominant research agendas) carries a heavy and depressing outlook.

Therefore, for us as teachers, scholars, and researchers conducting research with Latin@ and nondominant teachers weighs heavily on our consciousness. Certainly, the primary subtractive effect of not having equal representation of Latin@ practitioners in schools is on students. Our *testimonios* discuss numerous experiences where the absence of culturally meaningful pedagogy made us feel isolated and at odds with educational institutions. We call for more research that positions authentic Latin@ voices in positions to disrupt the *status quo* in teaching preparation and professional training. We unite our voices of resistance to those of

117

researchers promoting academic research agendas that bring forth authentic voices of nondominant teachers and that are committed to changing education in significant ways to meet the demands of our multi-racial, multi-ethnic, multi-lingual society (Antrop-González & De Jesús, 2006; Castro, 2010; DePalma, 2008; Kohli, 2008; 2009; Morrell, 2010; Nieto, 2005; Ochoa, 2007; Taliaferro Baszile, 2008). Our autobiographical work seeks to articulate Latina/o educators' voices from the front line and to document our efforts to eradicate racism, oppression, and social injustices in education for our communities. Unhooking from Whiteness is a work in progress for us and, as such, our work blends our personal and professional lives.

NOTES

[1] Latino: Throughout this chapter we use the term Latin@ instead of Hispanic, Latino/a, or Latino. However, is important to note that Latin@ defines heterogeneous groups that self-identify and identify others in terms of race and ethnicity such as Indígena, African, LatiNegro, White, Criollo, biracial, Mestizo, and Mulato (Amaro & Zambrana, 2000; Fergus, 2009). Other labels for self-identification include gender, ethnic background, place of birth in and out of the U.S., generational status in the context of immigration experiences, and linguistic skills in Spanish English, and indigenous tongues (Comas-Díaz, 2001; Fergus, 2009; Rivas-Drake, Hughes, & Way, 2009; Zentella, 1997).

REFERENCES

Amaro, H., & Zambrana, R. (2000). Criollo, mestizo, mulato, latinegro, indigena, white, or black? The US Hispanic/Latino population and multiple responses in the 2000 census. *American Journal of Public Health, 90*(11), 1724–1727.

Antrop-González, R., Vélez, W., & Garrett, T. (2005). ¿Dónde están los estudiantes puertorriqueños/as exitosos?: Success factors of high-achieving Puerto Rican high school students. *Journal of Latinos and Education, 4*(2), 77–94.

Antrop-González, R., & De Jesús, A. (2006). Towards a theory of critical care in urban small school reform: Examining structures and pedagogies of caring in two Latino community based schools. *International Journal of Qualitative Studies in Education, 19*(4), 409–433.

Bonilla-Silva, E. (2009). *Racism without racists: Color-bind racism and the persistence of racial inequality in America.* NY: Rowman & Littlefield Publishers.

Bourdieu, P., & Passeron, J. C. (1970). (Nice, R., Trans.) *Reproduction in education, society and culture* (Volume 5). London: Sage Publications.

Bourdieu, P. (1986). The forms of capital. In J. E. Richardson (Ed.) *Handbook of theory of research for the sociology of Education* (pp. 241–258). Greenword Press.

Bourdieu, P. (2003). *Language and symbolic power* (7th ed). *Cambridge, MA: Harvard University Press.*

Caminero-Santangelo, M. (2007). *On Latinidad: U.S. Latino literature and the construction of ethnicity.* University Press of Florida

Castro, A. (2010). Themes in the research on preservice teachers's views of culturally diversity: Implications for researching millennial preservice teachers. *Educational Research, 39*(3), 198–210.

Crawford, J. (1992). *Hold your tongue: Bilingualism and the politics of English-only.* Reading, Mass: Addison-Wesley.

Crawford, J., & Krashen, S. (2007). *English learners in American classrooms: 101 questions and 101 answers.* NY: Scholastic.

Cobas, J., & Feagin, J. (2008). Language oppression and resistance: The case of middle class Latinos in the United States. *Ethnic and Racial Studies, 31*(2), 390–410.

Comas-Díaz, L. (2001). Hispanics, Latinos, or Americanos: The evolution of identity. *Cultural Diversity and Ethnic Minority Psychology, 7*(2), 115–120.

Cox, M., Munro-Faure, P., Mathieu, P., Herrera, A., Palmer, D., & Groppo, P. (2003/2). FAO in Agrarian reform. *The food and agricultural organization of the United Nations.* Retrived from www.fao.org/DOCREP/006/J04515T/j0415t04.htm

DeGaetano, Y. (2007). The role of culture in engaging Latino parents involvement in school. *Urban Education, 42*(2), 145–162.

DeJesús, A., & Vasquez, D. W. (2005). Exploring the educational profile and pipeline for Latinos in New York state. *Centro de Estudios Puertorriqueños Hunter College (CUNY) Policy Brief, 2*(2), 10–11.

Delamont, S. (2009). The only honest thing: Autoethnography, reflexivity, and small crises in fieldwork. *Ethnography and Education, 4*(1), 51–63.

Delgado Bernal, D., Elenes, C. A., Godinez, F., & Villenas, S. (Eds.) (2006). *Chicana/Latina education in everyday life: Femenista perspectives on pedagogy and epistemology.* NY: State University of New York.

Delgado Bernal, D. (2008). La trenza de identidades: Weaving together my personal, professional, and communal identities. In K. P. Gonzalez & R. V. Padilla (Eds.) *Doing the public good: Latina/o scholars engage civic participation* (pp. 135–148). Sterling, VA: Stylus.

Delgado, R., & Stefancic, J. (2001). *Critical race theory: An introduction.* NY: New York University Press.

DePalma, R. (2008). The voice of every Black person?: Bringing authentic minority voices into the multicultural dialogue. *Teaching and Teacher Education, 24*, 767–778.

Duany, J., & Matos-Rodríguez, F. (2006). *Puerto Ricans in Orlando and Central Florida* (Vol. 1, No. 1). Centro de Estudios Puertorriqueños, Hunter College (CUNY).

Fergus, E. (2009). Understanding Latino students schooling experiences: The relevance of skin color among Mexican and Puerto Rican high school students. *Teachers College Record, 111*(2), 339–375.

Flores, J. (1993). *Divided borders: Essays on Puerto Rican identity.* Houston, TX: Arte Público Press.

Foucault, M. (1979/1984). *The Foucault reader.* New York: Pantheon.

Freire, P. (1990). *Pedagogy of the oppressed.* New York: Continuum.

Gardner, D., & Others (1983). A nation at risk: The imperative for educational reform. An open letter to the American people. *National Commission on Excellence in Education,* Dept. of Education Washington D.C. Retrieved from: http://eric.ed.gov/PDFS/ED226006.pdf

Gándara, P., & Contreras, F. (2010). *The Latino education crisis: The consequences of failed social policies.* Cambridge, Mass: Harvard University Press.

González, J. (2011). *Harvest of empire: A history of Latinos in America.* NY: Penguin.

Gonzáles, N., Moll, L., & Amanti, C. (2005). *Funds of knowledge: Theorizing practices in households, communities, and classrooms.* Mahwah, NJ: Lawrence Erlbaum Associates.

González, N. (2005). Beyond culture: The hybridity of funds of knowledge. In N. Gonzalez, L. Moll, & C. Amanti (Eds.) *Funds of knowledge: Theorizing practices in households, communities and classrooms* (pp. 29–46). Mahwah, NJ: Lawrence Erlbaum Associate.

Gutiérrez, K., Morales, P., & Martínez, D. (2009). Re-mediating literacy: culture, difference, and learning for students from nondominant communities. *Review of Research in Education, 33*, 212–245.

Harris, C. (1993). Whiteness as property. *Harvard Law Review, 106*(8), 1707.

Hughes, S., Pennington, J., & Makris, S. (2012). Translating autoethnography across the AERA standards: Toward understanding autoethnographic scholarship as empirical research. *Educational Researcher, 41*(6), 209–219.

Hurtado, A., & Gurin, P. (2004). *Chican/o identity in a changing U.S. society: The Mexican American experience.* AR: University of Arizona Press.

Irizarry, J., & Donaldson, M. (2012). Teach for America: The latinization of U.S. schools and the critical shortage of Latina/o teachers. *American Educational Research Journal, 49*(1), 155–194.

Kohli, R. (2008). Breaking the cycle of racism in the classroom: Critical race reflections from future teachers of color. *Teacher Education Quarterly, 35*(4), 177–188.

Kohli, R. (2009). Critical race reflections: Valuing the experiences of teachers of color in teacher education. *Race Ethnicity and Education, 12*(2), 235–251.

Kubota, R., & Lin, A. (Eds.) (2009). *Race, culture, and identities in second language education: Exploring critically engaged practice.* NY: Routledge.

119

Ladson-Bilings, G., & Tate, W. (1995). Toward a critical race theory of education. *Teachers College Records, 97*(1), 47–68.

Ladson Bilings, G. (2005). *Beyond the big house: African American educators on teaching and education.* NY: Teacher College Press.

Lantolf, J., & Sunderman, G. (2001). The struggle for a place in the sun: Rationalizing foreign language study in the twentieth century. *The Modern Language Journal, 85*(1), 5–25.

Libienski, S. T. (2003). Celebrating diversity and denying disparities: A critical assessment. *Educational Researcher, 32*(30), 30–38.

Lucas, T. (Ed.) (2011). *Teacher preparation for linguistically diverse classrooms: A resource for teacher educators.* NY: Routledge.

Luria, H., Seymour, D., & Smoke, T. (Eds.) (2006). *Language and linguistics in context: Readings and applications for teachers.* Mahwah, NJ: Lawrence Erlbaum

Kiyama, J. M. (2010). College aspirations and limitations. *American Educational Research Journal, 47*(2), 330–356.

Martín Alcoff, L. (2006). *Visible identities: Race, gender, and self.* Oxford: Oxford University Press.

Macaluso, T. L. (2010, April 7). Education: The color of education. *City Newspaper.* Retrieved from: http://www.rochestercitynewspaper.com/news/articles/2010/04/EDUCATION-the-color-of-education/

Milos, P. (2004). CIDE 40 años. *Publicación del Centro de Investigación y Desarrollo de la Educación (CIDE).* Retrieved from: Biblioteca.uahurtado.cl/ujah/reduc/pdf/mfn309.pdf

Monkman, K., Ronald, M., & Théramène, F. D. (2005). Social and cultural capital in an urban Latino school community. *Urban Education, 40*(4), 4–33.

Morrell, J. (2010). Teacher preparation and diversity: When American pre-service teachers aren't White and middle class. *International Journal of Multicultural Education, 12*(1), 1–17.

Mulkey, L. (1993). Chapter 7 – Stratification: Rules for acquiring the desirable things in life. In Mulkey Lynn (Ed.) *Sociology of education: Theoretical and empirical investigations.* New York: Harcourt Brace.

Murillo, E., Villenas, S., Galván, R. T., Sánchez Muñoz, J., Martínez, C., & Machado-Casas, (Eds.) (2010). *Handbook of Latinos and education: Theory, research, and practice.* NY: Routledge.

NCES (2009). *Report on Staffing Survey from 2007–2008.* Retrieved from: http://nces.ed.gov/pubs2009/2009324/tables/sass0708_2009324_t12n_02.asp

NCES (2011). *Projections of education Statistics to 2020* (39th Ed.). Retrieved from: http://nces.ed.gov/pubs2011/2011026.pdf

NCES (2011b). *The Condition of Education 2011.* Retrieved from: http://nces.ed.gov/pubsearch/pubsinfo.asp?pubid=2011033

Nieto, S. (2002). *Language, culture, and teaching: Critical perspectives for a new century.* Mahwah, NJ: Lawrence Erlbaum.

Nieto, S. (2005). *Why we teach.* NY: Teacher College Press.

Nguniri, F., Hernandez, K., & Chang, H. (2010). Living autoethnography: Connecting life and research. *Journal of Research Practice, 6*(1), Article E1. Retrieved from: Http://jrp.icaap.org/index.php/jrp/article/view/24/186.

Ochoa, G. (2007). *Learning from Latino teachers.* CA: Jossey-Bass.

Olneck, M. (2000). Can multicultural education change what counts as cultural capital? *American Educational Research Journal, 37*(2), 317–348.

Oughton, H.(2010) Funds of knowledge: A conceptual critique. *Studies in the Education of Adults, 42*(1), 63–78.

Pennycook, A. (2010). *Language as a local practice.* NY: Routledge.

Pérez -Huber, L. P. (2009). Challenging racist nativist framing: Acknowledging the community cultural wealth of undocumented Chicana college students to reframe the immigration debate. *Harvard Educational Review, 79*(4), 704–729.

Portes, A. (1998). Social capital: Its origins and applications in modern sociology. *Annual Review of Sociology, 24,* 1–24.

Portes, A. (2000). Two meanings of social capital. *Sociological Forum, 15*(1), 1–12.

Reagan, T. (2009). *Language matters: Reflections on educational linguistics.* Charlotte, NC: Information Age Publishing, Inc.

Rios-Aguilar, C., Kiyama, JM., Gravitt, M., & Moll, L (2011). Funds of knowledge for the poor and forms of capital for the rich? A capital approach to examining funds of knowledge. *Theory and Research in Education, 9*(2), 163–184.

Rivas-Drake, D., Hughes, D., & Way, N. (2009). Public ethnic regard and perceived socioeconomic stratification: Associations with well-being among dominican and black American youth. *Journal of Early Adolescence, 29*(1), 122–141.

Rogoff, B. (2003). *The cultural nature of human development.* Oxford: Oxford University Press.

Sánchez, P., & Machado-Casas, M. (2009). At the intersection of transnationalism, Latina/o immigrants, and education. *The High School Journal, 92*(4), 3–15.

San Miguel, G. (2011). Embracing Latinidad: Beyond nationalism in the history of Education. *Journal of Latinos and Education, 10*(1), 3–22.

Santa Ana, O. (Ed.) (2004). *Tongue-tied: The lives of multilingual children in public school.* NY: Rowman & Littlefield Publishers.

Solórzano, D., & Delgado Bernal, D. (2001). Examining transformational resistance through a critical race and Latcrit theory framework: Chicana and Chicano students in an urban context. *Urban Education, 36*(3), 308–342.

Spring, J. (2008). *American education.* Boston: McGraw Hill.

Springer, J. (2009). *Deculturalization and the struggle for equality: A brief history of the education of dominated cultures in the United States.* Boston: McGraw-Hill.

Stampnitzky, L. (2006). How does "culture" become "capital"? Cultural and intuitional struggles over "character and personality" at Harvard. *Sociological Perspectives, 49*(4), 461–481.

Suárez-Orozco, M., & Páez, M. (Eds.) (2009). *Latinos: Remaking America.* Berkeley, CA: University of California Press.

Taliaferro Baszile, D. (2008). The oppressor within: A counterstory of race, repression, and teacher reflection. *Urban Review, 40*, 371–385.

Tellez, K. (2004). Preparing teachers for Latino children and youth: Policies and practice. *The High School Journal, 88*(2), 43–54.

Tyke, B (2000). Chapter 1- Defining the deep structure of schooling. In *Hard truths: Uncovering the deep structure of schooling* (pp. 12–24). New York: Teachers College Press.

Urrieta, L. (2009). *Working from within: Chicana and Chicano activist educators in Whitestream schools.* AR: University of Arizona Press.

Valdés, G. (2001). Heritage language students: Profiles and possibilities. In J. Kreeft Peyton, D. Ranard, A., & S. McGinnis (Eds.) *Heritage Languages in America: Preserving a national resource.* McHenry, IL: Delta Systems.

Valdés, G., Gonzáles, S., López García, D., & Márquez, P. (2003). Language ideology: The case of Spanish in departments of foreign language. *Anthropology & Education Quarterly, 38*(1), 3–26.

Valdés, G., Fishman, J., Chávez, R., & Pérez, W. (2008). *Developing minority language resources: The case of Spanish in California.* Bilingual Education and Bilingualism 58. Clevedon: Multilingual Matters. University Press.

Valenzuela, A. (1999). *Subtractive schooling: U.S. Mexican youth and the politics of caring.* NY: State University of New York Press.

Villenas, S. (2009). Knowing and unknowing transnational Latino lives in teacher education: At the intersection of educational research and the Latino humanities. *The High School Journal, 92*(4), 129–136.

Yosso, T. (2005). Whose culture has capital? A critical race theory discussion of community cultural wealth. *Race Ethnicity and Education, 8*(1), 69–91.

Yosso, T. (2006). *Critical Race counterstories along the Chicana/Chicano educational pipeline.* NY: Routledge.

Yosso, T., Smith, W., Ceja, M., & Solórzano, D. (2009). Critical race theory, racial microaggressions and campus racial climate for Latina/o undergraduates. *Harvard Educational Review, 79*(4), 659–691.

Zentella, A. C. (1997). *Growing up bilingual: Puerto Rican children in New York.* Malden, Mass: Blackwell Publishers.

Zentella, A. C. (Ed.) (2005). *Building on strength: Language and literacy in Latino families and communities.* New York: Teacher College Press.

NICHOLAS D. HARTLEP & CLEVELAND HAYES

9. INTERRUPTING THE RACIAL
TRIANGULATION OF ASIANS

Unhooking from Whiteness as a Form of Coalitional Politics

> ...while Asian Americans and African Americans are fighting among themselves, the racial barriers that limit Asian Americans and African Americans remain unchallenged.
>
> —Lee (1996), p. 9

Asian Americans are considered to be "honorary" Whites (Tuan, 1998). This means that they are positioned as middlemen within the existing Black-White racial binary. In this racial binary, Asian Americans are triangulated between African Americans and Whites. The racial triangulation of Asian Americans as racial middlemen and also as academic "model minorities" make them an extremely vulnerable population for "being used" by Whiteness. Indeed, Matsuda (2010) warns that Asian Americans need to be cautious in order not to be "used" by White supremacy, and Delgado (1991) similarly warns Asian Americans from becoming used as majoritarian role models. Kim (1998) argues that being positioned as a "model" minority validates the notion that the United States is a colorblind society. Asian Americans having a higher educational attainment and income than Latin@ or African Americans is presented by the dominant group as evidence for this notion. In order to justify its preference for race-neutral policies, the dominant culture points to indices in which Asian Americans are presumably doing well. The narrative can be summarized as follows: If Asian Americans can succeed, why cannot others such as African Americans and Latin@s? Kim (1998) points out that the mainstream spotlights the belief that Asian Americans succeed without programs such as affirmative action and bilingual education; programs that, when accessed, have been used to accuse Latin@s and African Americans of being lazy and dependent.

Juxtaposing Asian Americans with African Americans and Latin@s serves to absolve the privileged in society from being held responsible for the oppressive and dehumanizing impact of White supremacy on the lives of other people of color. In her article, Kim (1998) argues that this "racially-triangulated" position is dangerous for Asian Americans, especially if they do not understand what this position means within the larger context of power/race relations. In addition to the importance of understanding the racial triangulation of Asian Americans in order to understand how coalitional politics is important for antiracist work, several scholars have asked

C. Hayes and N.D. Hartlep (Eds.), Unhooking from Whiteness:
The Key to Dismantling Racism in the United States, 123–130.
© *2013 Sense Publishers. All Rights Reserved.*

relevant questions. Devos and Banaji (2005) ask, Does "American = White?" and Zhou (2004) asks, "Are Asian Americans becoming White?"

PURPOSE OF COALITIONAL POLITICS

The growth of Asian Americans in the United States is a demographic certainty. Thus, a question that social scientists ask in their research is whether or not these increases in people of color in the United States will breed hostility or harmony (Davidson, Fielden, & Omar, 2010 Dixon, 2006; Kim 1998). The major argument is that when there are large numbers of people of color in one particular area, it arouses White anxiety, and historically, as DuBois (1935) has argued, Whites have created structures and a racial hierarchy as a mechanism to keep people from joining forces. Consequently, one effective way to disrupt racial triangulation is through formulating coalitions that problematize Whiteness and the privileges that come with being White.

Just as Whites did at the end of the Civil War, between freed slaves and poor Whites, White supremacy has created a tension between Asian Americans and Black Americans by placing Asian Americans higher on the racial "pecking" order, making them the "model minority" or "honorary White." This perceived social hierarchy created by White supremacy consequently keeps Blacks and Asians at odds with one another, thus preserving White supremacy (Bikmen, 2011; Bonilla-Silva, 2004; Du Bois, 1935; Kim, 1998; Lee, 2005).

We argue that there is an urgent need for Black-Asian coalitional politics (Aoki, 2010). In other words, given that White supremacy divides-and-conquers non-White minorities, it is incumbent that African Americans and Asian Americans form socio-political coalitions in order to fight for racial justice. Implications for such politics are shared. Such coalition-building forces Whites to realize that racism is not only about having prejudicial feelings about people of color. It is also about the systems that are in place to keep one group of people at odds with another to make sure the structures maintain White privilege do not come tumbling down (hooks, 1992; Kim, 1998 Leonardo, 2009).

HOW RACIAL TRIANGULATION WORKS

Figure 9.1 illustrates the racial triangulation of Whites, Asians, and African Americans. In her article "The Racial Triangulation of Asian Americans," Kim (1999) identifies what we feel is a compelling and functional theoretical model for the idea that unhooking from Whiteness will lead to termination of racial triangulation. Both of our journeys of unhooking from Whiteness, while different, have had the same effect: a desire to become active agents of antiracism.

We argue that the divide-and-conquer function of Whiteness has prevented African and Asian Americans from working together in fighting their common

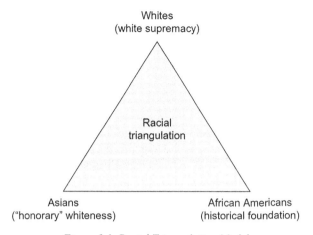

Figure 9.1. Racial Triangulation Model

plight. We affirm that through coalitional politicking, unhooking from Whiteness is the key to doing antiracist work in the United States.

White racial framing is more than a deeply embedded cognitive tool historically used by Whites (Picca & Feagin, 2007; Feagin, 2010); it is a collectively shared perspective that guides how Whites as individuals and groups think about and interact with people of color (Feagin, 2010; Gillborn, 2005; Leonardo, 2005). The White racial frame is a guide and therefore does not determine how Whites as individuals or groups, or anyone else using the knowledge of Whiteness, will act. As we learn more about the functions and consequences of White racial knowledge in structuring the distribution of education, we may become better equipped to interrupt the processes of race-based dominance, which will continue to produce inequalities in education.

CRITICAL RACE THEORY

Like Knaus (2009), we have employed critical race theory (CRT) in this book for the purpose of developing the voices and narratives that challenge racism and the structures of oppression while advocating for social justice in its many forms (Hartlep, 2010). Tate (1997) asked the question, "Pivotal in understanding CRT as a methodology, what role should experiential knowledge of race, class and gender play in educational discourse?" (p. 235). Ladson-Billings (1998) states that CRT focuses on the role of "voice in bringing additional power and experiential knowledge that people of color speak regarding the fact that our society is deeply structured by racism" (p. 13). In a similar vein, Solórzano and Yosso (2001) define CRT as "an attempt to understand the oppressive aspects of society in order to generate societal and individual transformation and [it is] important for educators to understand that

CRT is different from any other theoretical framework because it centers race" (p. 471–472). As a result, CRT scholars have developed the following tenets to guide CRT research and all of these tenets are utilized within the design and analysis of this chapter and volume (Kohli, 2009):

Centrality of Race and Racism

All CRT research within education must centralize race and racism, as well as acknowledge the intersection of race with other forms of subordination (Kohli, 2009; Sleeter & Delgado Bernal, 2002). As our narratives showed, CRT is our way to interpret and de-center Whiteness in the larger society. In order to forge partnerships in the fight for social justice, we also had to begin a critique of our own Whiteness. We did this by first de-centering Whiteness from our own lives.

Valuing Experiential Knowledge

Solórzano and Yosso (2001) argue that CRT in educational research recognizes that the experiential knowledge of students of color is legitimate, appropriate, and critical to understanding, analyzing, and teaching about racial subordination in the field of education. Life stories tend to be accurate according to the perceived realities of subjects' lives. They are used to elicit structured stories and detailed lives of the individuals involved (Delgado, 1989; McCray, Sindelar, Kilgore, & Neal, 2002).

Fairbanks (1996) states that storytelling, one of the methodologies of CRT, has been an accepted mode of constructing realities throughout human history. CRT narratives and storytelling provide readers with a challenging account of preconceived notions of race. The thick descriptions that emerged from the stories in his volume served to illuminate the experiences of the person telling the story (Parker & Lynn, 2002). Stories offer descriptions and explanations of situations and circumstances from which readers may cull insights into their own practices. For example, storytelling is about human agents doing things on the basis of beliefs and desires, striving for goals, and meeting obstacles (Fairbanks, 1996).

Challenging the Dominant Perspective

CRT research works to challenge dominant narratives, often referred to as majoritarian stories. CRT scholar Harris (1995) describes the "valorization of Whiteness as treasured property in a society structured on racial caste" (p. 277). Harris (1995) also argues that Whiteness conferred tangible and economically valuable benefits, and it was jealously guarded as a valued possession. This thematic strand of Whiteness as property in the United States is not confined to the nation's early history (Frankenberg, 1993; Ladson-Billings, 1998).

In line with the thesis of this chapter—interrupting racial triangulation—"unhooking from Whiteness" for us means centering the problem of White racism and refusing to place the onus on communities of color to fix the problem that they did not create. Whiteness, which were seen in our narratives, caused both of us to take ownership of "fixing" our communities, in hopes of obtaining some sort of validation. "Unhooking from Whiteness," for people of color, forces Whites to move away from a discourse of White racism to a discourse of Whiteness because White racism is inherently oppressive while Whiteness is multifaceted and complex (Hayes & Juárez, 2009; Kendall, 2006; Leonardo, 2009).

Commitment to Social Justice

Social justice must always be a motivation behind CRT research. Part of this social justice commitment must include a critique of liberalism, claims of neutrality, objectivity, color blindness and meritocracy as a camouflage for the self-interest of powerful entities of society (Tate, 1997). Only aggressive, color-conscious efforts to change the way things are done will do much to ameliorate misery (Delgado & Stefancic, 2001; Tate, 1997).

Being Interdisciplinary

According to Tate (1997), CRT crosses epistemological boundaries. It borrows from several traditions, including liberalism, feminism, and Marxism to include a more complete analysis of "raced" people. Ladson-Billings (1998) has already put forth the argument that CRT has a place within education. She argues that CRT in education allows for the use of parables, chronicles, stories, and counterstories to illustrate the false necessity and irony of much of current civil rights doctrine: we really have not gone as far as we think we have. Adopting CRT as a framework for educational equity means that we will have to expose racism in education and propose radical solutions for addressing the ever-present issue (Ladson-Billing, 1998).

In this book's concluding chapter we write that we believe that both groups—Blacks and Asians—don't necessarily have to become "pawns" of Whiteness (Leonardo, 2010), but in order to fight co-option this requires them both to "unhook" from Whiteness. If we give "honorary White" status to Asian Americans, they will perpetuate Black racism. But if Asian (Korean) Americans, like Hartlep, unhook from Whiteness, that is, if they refuse to be used by White supremacy, they will be able to fight for antiracism. The divide-and-conquer strategy that Whiteness uses must be interrupted in order to stop racism, once and for all.

For instance, Shrake (2006, p. 183) states that the model minority stereotype is "a politically divisive tool" and that "the model minority image produces a specific minority position within the hegemonic racial structure in American society; one level lower than Whites and one level higher than other minorities" (p. 184).

Hegemony can only stop when minorities and Whites unhook from Whiteness, and refuse to abide by the racial stratification of non-White minorities.

THE ACADEMY: LIFE AS AN ASIAN AMERICAN ASSISTANT PROFESSOR

Now, as an Assistant Professor of Educational Foundations, Hartlep is reticent toward the notion that all White anti-racists are allies and want what's best for his own life (Gorski, 2012). Iijima (1998) writes that oppressors at times strategically appear as if they want to be allies and assist oppressed people. According to Iijima (1998), "In order to have the continued opportunity to express their 'generosity,' the oppressors [White supremacy] must perpetuate injustice as well" (p. 385). Progress for Asian Americans will only be made with active Asian American resistance. Oppressors do this because they want to maintain their position as dominator. Bell (1980) called this "interest convergence"—when Whites will assist marginalized people of color whenever there is a convergence with their own ulterior interests.

As an Asian American Assistant Professor, it is Hartlep's understanding that he must utilize his titular privilege—Dr.—as a way to assist folks of color who are not as fortunate as he is. To borrow from Duncan-Andrade (2009), his professional and personal mission is to steal as much soil as he can from the ivory tower and return it to its proper place—the communities of color—which have many roses growing in the concrete. In some ways he grew in the concrete—and in other ways, his avoidance of being used by Whiteness as a pawn is his way of "unhooking" from Whiteness.

Asian Americans represent a critical mass of people: they are the fastest growing minority group, constitute a population with $254.6 billion buying power, and are a young population (Taylor, Landreth, & Bang, 2005). African Americans have a long and rich history of resistance. As chattel slaves, African Americans staged numerous revolts that have been successful. This is why African Americans constitute the historical foundation upon which Asian Americans can lean and learn.

As a recently tenured professor, Hayes now has more academic freedom to do the important work that he was unable to do as a pre-tenure Black professor. Hayes is the first African American to receive tenure at LaVerne, something he is constantly reminded of when he enters the space of higher education. It is called the ivory tower for a reason—Whiteness.

UNHOOKING FROM WHITENESS: A CRITICAL RACE PERSPECTIVE

By using counter-narratives, our attempt in this book was to interrupt Whiteness by "unhooking from it." We conclude this volume with the idea that racial triangulation is insidious and that unhooking from Whiteness should include building coalitions in hopes of ending racism in the United States. Whiteness continues to prosper when it keeps marginalized groups at odds with each other.

As previously mentioned, this discourse can be seen in a historical context after the Civil War. When the Civil War ended, DuBois (1935) argues that White land owners created a social order that prevented poor Whites from joining political forces with the freed slaves. We hope that our counter-stories will disrupt that social divide between Asian Americans and African Americans for the greater good.

The first step, in order for us to unhook from Whiteness and begin to interrupt racial triangulation, is to hone the ability to understand that racism is an endemic part of American society. However, the problem with Whites and some people of color is their refusal to consider the everyday realities of race and racism (Bergerson, 2003; Dei, Karumanchery and Karumanchery-Luik; 2007; Gillborn, 2005; Leonardo, 2010).

Second, we must grapple with the idea that there is no such thing as colorblindness *per se*. According to Bergerson (2003), Whites attribute negative stereotypes to people of color while at the same time espousing their opposition to blatant racism. When White liberals fail to understand how they can and do embody White supremacist values even though they themselves may not embrace racism through this lack of awareness, they support the racist domination they wish to eradicate (Gillborn, 2005; hooks, 1989).

Third, we must understand that meritocracy, like colorblindness, does not exist. It is not enough to say that anyone who works hard can achieve success. Students of color are systematically excluded from education and educational opportunities despite their hard work. Merit operates under the burden of racism; racism thus limits the applicability of merit to people of color (Bergerson, 2003). The hard work of some pays off much more than the hard work of racial others.

Lastly, unhooking from Whiteness requires us to understand the property value of Whiteness. Whiteness was invented and continues to be maintained to serve as the dominant and normal status against which racial *others* are measured. Whiteness serves to make these "others" less privileged, less powerful, and less legitimate.

IMPLICATIONS FOR UNHOOKING FROM WHITENESS

Coalition building is not easy, and unhooking from Whiteness is especially difficult for those individuals who have grown up in an environment that clouds one's view of the world through the notion of meritocracy and liberalism: If a person just works hard then the phenotype of the person does not matter. However, the process is not mutually exclusive. Kim (1998) argues that coalition building should not be viewed as a site for comfort and refuge, but as a site for struggle.

The fact is that with the increased visibility of Asian Americans comes the responsibility that Asian Americans can no longer be dismissed as "honorary" Whites. Asians, similar to African Americans, American Indians, and Latin@s, are facing enormous challenges such as the assault on the poor, immigration challenges, and blatant racial attack: see the YouTube video made by a UCLA White student towards Asians on the campus. Kim (1998) asks the question, "With whom will we join forces?" (p. 11). It is through this research that we can find ways to hold the upholders and functionaries of the *status quo* accountable for creating this "buffer zone" that places Asians between mostly White people who have the power to make the rules and those mostly Black and Brown people who are oppressed by them (Bikmen, 2001; Dhingra, 2003; Kim, 1998)

Sometimes unhooking from Whiteness will cause a person to lose advantage. This can be seen in Hayes's (cf. Chapter 2 of this volume) notion of "academic lynching." Before people "unhook" they surely buy into the idea that a meritocracy exists. Believing that if people just work harder they'll achieve their lot is these peoples' defense mechanism or strategy to defend against racism, if you will. Sadly, though, acquiescence is like "colorblindness"; it fails to recognize and analyze power. By acquiescing to racism, people (of color and Whites) in turn become disempowered and "defined" by racism, rather than the definers of their own lives. Thus, acquiescing causes non-Whites to lose power. Unhooking from Whiteness might cause someone to lose power, but at least they maintain the power to define themselves.

REFERENCES

Aoki, A. L. (2010). Coalition Politics. In E. W. Chen & G. J. Yoo (Eds.) *Encyclopedia of Asian American issues today* (volume 2) (pp. 707–712). Santa Barabara, CA: Greenwood Press.

Bell, D. A. (1980). Brown v. Board of education and the Interest-Convergence Dilemma. *Harvard Law Review, 93*(3), 518–533.

Bergerson, A. A. (2003). Critical race theory and white racism: is there room for White scholars in fighting racism in education? *Qualitative Studies in Education, 16*(1), 51–63.

Bikmen, N. (2011). Asymmetrical effects of contact between minority groups: Asian and Black students in small college. *Cultural Diversity and Ethnic Minority Psychology, 17*(2), 186–194.

Chae, Y. (2008). Cultural Economies of Model Minority Creation. In Y. Chae, (Ed.) *Politicizing Asian American literature: Towards a critical multiculturalism* (pp. 19–30). New York, NY: Routledge.

Choi, D. H. (1992, Spring). The other side of the model minority myth. *Yisei Magazine, 5*(2), 20–23, 25, 26. A digitized copy is available here: http://www.hcs.harvard.edu/~yisei/issues/spring_92/ys92_20.html

Dei, G. J. S., Karumanchery, L. L., & Karumanchery-Luik, N. (2007). *Playing the race card: Exposing White power and privilege.* New York, NY: Peter Lang.

Delgado, R. (1991). Affirmative action as a Majoritarian Device: Or, do you really want to be a role model? *Michigan Law Review, 89*(5), 1222–1231.

Devos, T., & Banaji, M. R. (2005). American = White? *Journal of Personality and Social Psychology, 88*(3), 447–466.

Dhingra, P. H. (2003). Being American between black and white: Second generation Asian American professionals racial identities. *Journal of Asian American Studies, 6*(2), 117–147.

Dixon, J. C. (2006). The ties that bind and those that don't: Toward reconciling group threat and contact theories of prejudice. Social Forces, *84*(4), 2179–2203.

DuBois, W. E. B. (1935). *Black reconstruction in America: 1860–1880.* New York: The Free Press.

Duncan-Andrade, J. M. R. (2009). Note to educators: Hope required when growing roses in concrete. *Harvard Educational Review, 79*(2), 181–194.

Freire, P., & Macedo, D. (1987). *Literacy: Reading the word and the world.* Westport, CT: Greenwood Publishing.

Fujino, D. C. (2008). Who studies the Asian American movement? A historiographical analysis. *Journal of Asian American Studies, 11*(2), 127–169.

Gillborn, D. (2005). Education policy as an act of white supremacy: Whiteness, critical race theory and education reform. *Journal of Education Policy, 20*(4), 485–505.

Gorski, P. (2012, February 6). Complicating White privilege: Poverty, class, and the nature of the knapsack. *Teachers College Record.* http://www.tcrecord.org ID Number: 16687

Hartlep, N. D. (2010). *Going public: Critical race theory and issues of social justice.* Mustang, OK: Tate.

hooks, b. (1992). *Black looks: Race and representation.* Boston: South End Press.

hooks, b. (1989). *Talking back: Thinking feminist, thinking black*. Boston, MA: South End Press.

Iijima, C. K. (1998). Reparations and the "model minority" ideology of acquiescence: The necessity to refuse the return to original humiliation. *Boston College Law Review, 40*(1), 385–427.

Kim, C. J. (1999). The racial triangulation of Asian Americans. *Politics & Society, 27*(1), 105–138.

Kim, E. (1998). At least you're not black: Asian Americans in U.S. race relations. *Social Justice, 25*(3), 3–19.

Lee, S. J. (2005). *Up against Whiteness: Race, school, and immigrant youth*. New York, NY: Teachers College Press.

Lee, S., Juon, H., Martinez, G., Hsu, C. E., Robinson, E. S., Bawa, J., & Ma, G. X. (2009). Model Minority at risk: Expressed needs of mental health by Asian American Young Adults. *Journal of Community Health, 34*(2), 144–152.

Leonardo, Z. (2010). *Race, Whiteness and education*. New York: Routledge.

Lin-Fu, J. S. (1988). Population characteristics and health care needs of Asian Pacific Americans. *Public Health Reports, 103*(1), 18–27.

Loewen, J. W. (1988). *The Mississippi Chinese: Between black and white*. Prospect Heights, IL: Waveland Press.

Matsuda, M. J. (2010). We will not be used: Are Asian Americans the racial bourgeoisie? In J. S. Wu & T. C. Chen (Eds.) *Asian American studies now: A critical reader* (pp. 558–564). New Brunswick, NJ: Rutgers University Press.

Rothenberg, P. S. (2002). *White privilege: Essential readings on the other side of racism*. New York, NY: Worth Publishers

Royster, D. A. (2003*). Race and the invisible hand: How white networks exclude black men from blue-collar Jobs*. Berkeley, CA: University of California Press. Shim, D. (1998). From Yellow Peril Through Model Minority to Renewed Yellow Peril. *Journal of Communication Inquiry, 22*(4), 385–409.

Shrake, E. K. (2006). Unmasking the self: Struggling with the model minority stereotype and lotus blossom image. In G. Li & G. H. Beckett (Eds.) *"Strangers" of the academy: Asian women scholars in higher education* (pp. 178–194). Sterling, VA: Stylus.

Solórzano, D. G., & Yosso, T. J. (2002). Critical race methodology: Counter-storytelling as an analytical framework for education research. *Qualitative Inquiry, 8*(1), 23–44.

Tayag, M. (2011, Spring). Great expectations: The negative consequences and policy implications of the Asian American "Model Minority" Stereotype. *Stanford Journal of Asian American Studies, 4*, 23–31.

Taylor, C. R., Landreth, S., & Bang, H. (2005). Asian Americans in magazine advertising: Portrayals of the "model minority." *Journal of Macromarketing, 25*(2), 163–174.

Tuan, M. (1998). *Forever foreigners or honorary whites?: The Asian ethnic experience today*. New Brunswick, NJ: Rutgers University Press.

Zhou, M. (2004). Are Asian Americans becoming "white?" *Contexts, 3*(1), 29–37.

JOY L. LEI

AFTERWORD

SHARDS OF WHITENESS: ON BEING AN ASIAN AMERICAN
CHIEF DIVERSITY OFFICER

"Have you thought about how your race played a role in why you were hired?"

Less than three weeks after I started my job as University of La Verne's first Chief Diversity and Inclusivity Officer, an African American faculty member asked me this question. I appreciated his bluntness for asking the question that was probably in the minds of other individuals of color on this campus. It is certainly a question that has crossed my mind, although not for the first time in my career. It is a question that highlights the deceptive positioning of Asian Americans in relation to other populations of color, in relation to Whiteness. I thought about how this question would have different meanings if posed to a Black or Latino Chief Diversity Officer (CDO), if it would be posed at all. This question also put me in a dilemma—if I recognized that I had an advantage as an Asian American, does that mean I do not deserve the job? Would the implication be that only African Americans (and maybe Latin@s) can legitimately be CDOs?

"Yes," I responded, "and I plan to use it to my advantage."

As an Asian American in U.S. society, my positionality is a constant struggle between where I see myself and where others place me. I am/am not a person of color; I am/am not White; I am/am not oppressed; I face/don't face racism; and I have/don't have privilege (and maybe even power). Where I get placed, depending on the situation, is always to the benefit of Whiteness. Maybe I was hired because I am seen as the model minority—non-threatening and not overly aggressive, won't rock the boat, and will go along with the wishes of the majority—or because I have been granted "honorary White" status—with my skin color being closer to that of the rest of senior management, a person of color but more "like us." Of course, I was also hired because of my qualifications and experience. But I realize my Asianness and femaleness are part of the package. How they are significant, however, differs depending on who is judging and reacting to these identities.

My response to the question reflected my defensiveness towards the implication that I got this job because my skin color made me more agreeable to the White majority. It also reflected my eagerness to let the faculty member know that I "get it" and will beat the dominant structure at its own game to work towards a diverse, inclusive and equitable institution. It takes advocacy and resilience in the face of barriers and opposition, and I wanted/needed to prove that an Asian American can be a successful CDO.

I used to (half) joke that I am a recovering model minority. Can Whiteness be an addiction? If it can be, then it is just as destructive for the addict and those around them. The chapters in this book have helped me better define my journey to unhook from Whiteness, at least where I am now. The theories and analyses within the authors' narratives of their journeys undergird this afterword. What I face are shards of Whiteness—not a complete reflection of Whiteness, but sharp pieces of it in varying sizes. I never saw a complete, undamaged reflection. (Can any person of color?) As a child immigrant who arrived not speaking a word of English, my otherness was tacked onto me from the start. However, back then the reflection was intact, only cracked into big parts. Whiteness, albeit a distorted version of it, stared back at me and showed me what I looked like—yellow, short, slanted eyes—and what I was like—quiet, submissive, exotic. As a young person, I wanted to be whole, not realizing that this desire had to do with Whiteness. Subconsciously thinking I could never be White with my inseparable foreignness, I turned my attention to being the model minority because it was a "positive" role and one that allowed me to belong. Look at all the advantages, accomplishments, and accolades I get! I may face racism through taunts and threats and ostracism, and others who look like me have been through much worse, *but at least we don't have it as bad as they do.*

I shattered that reflection of Whiteness into broken pieces, wanting to do away with it when my consciousness was raised in graduate school and I learned to name that reflection as Whiteness and to understand its insidious and hegemonic nature. But the shards are still scattered on the floor, and the untouchable jagged pieces of Whiteness glimmer at me, reminding me that I will always see Whiteness within me.

When I was in my master's program, my advisor got together her students whose research topics were about race, and we met periodically to discuss an article or each other's research. I was very excited to be in this group, not only for the intellectual stimulation but more to be among individuals who shared the same commitment to social justice and racial equity. During our second gathering and a discussion about an article on Critical Race Theory, I connected the article to the experiences of Asian Americans. A fellow student, whom I admired and who is a Black woman, responded, in brief, that she did not think the article was relevant to Asian Americans and that centering race meant focusing on the racism experienced by Blacks. I felt my face flush and my body tremble from feeling belittled. I didn't say anything because the incident made me feel I did not have legitimate claim to experiencing racism. The next day, I ran into another student in the group, who is a Hawaiian woman, and she brought up that discussion. She said her understanding is that, to conquer racism in U.S. society, we need to focus on the experiences of African Americans because they have it the worst, and if we can eliminate racism towards Black Americans, then we will have eliminated racism as a whole. I told her that there must be room to address the different forms of racism towards different people and that this is needed to understand fully how racism works. By only focusing on the racism towards one group, we will not address the different ways that racism plays out in, for example, her community. I listed examples of the racism she had previously shared that her community experienced, and pointed out how they would not be addressed if we only focused on the experiences of African Americans. Still, the message that what

Asian Americans experience is not really racism or is not as bad as what other groups experience was strong and clear.

Asian Americans are not considered an underrepresented minority, even though this umbrella term conceals an enormous diversity of ethnicities, immigration histories, socioeconomic class backgrounds, and academic and professional achievement. Some have referred to Asian Americans as "honorary Whites," but this framework maintains the Black/White binary—if you're not Black, you must be White. Yellow, if you will, is its own thing. At a micro, day-to-day level, it can seem as if Asian Americans have privilege and power (when compared to the stereotypes of other populations of color and if you only focus on successful people), but what is masked as privilege and power actually serve to strengthen White supremacy and place Asian Americans in a precarious position, pitting them against other populations of color, creating animosity rather than coalitions. It conceals the various forms of racism faced by Asian Americans. We need a more complicated understanding of and language for U.S. race relations in order to untangle the ways Whiteness threads through our lives.

Stereotypes of Asian Americans, Blacks/African Americans, Latin@s, and Native Americans are believed not only by Whites but by the various populations of color as well. These mutual stereotypes come to a head in situations, for example, where there are Asian American store owners in largely African American and Latino neighborhoods. The Asians are seen as coming into Black and Latino neighborhoods and taking advantage of their customers, all the while acting rude and hiding behind bullet proof windows. The Blacks and Latin@s are seen as dangerous, dirty, and always shoplifting, just waiting for the opportunity to loot the stores like they did during the L.A. Riots. I do not have the space to even begin to unravel the racist social and economic circumstances that lead to there being low-income, predominantly Black and Latino neighborhoods with Asian store owners who will not live in those neighborhoods. This racial dynamic, seen in different contexts but always among populations of color, is an example of how Whiteness maintains its power and privilege. This destructive prejudice is a tool of White racism—it keeps us fighting amongst ourselves instead of against the power of Whiteness.

It is important to understand and counteract the insidious effects of Whiteness on relationships among populations of color. Too often these effects are skirted to avoid division and to maintain a unified front with people of color against Whites (where do Asian Americans fit in here?). While skirting prejudice among populations of color may seem to be a way to keep peace and build coalitions, it maintains the Black/White binary and keeps us from understanding how Whiteness works in more complicated and nuanced ways. We need to acknowledge there is prejudice among populations of color, understand how this prejudice maintains White supremacy, *and* build coalitions and work successfully together. We know the power and privilege Whiteness bestows on Whites, *and* we can work with White allies who do the hard work of understanding and counteracting their privilege and power, using them strategically as well to fight against White supremacy.

Recently, I was at a conference for the National Association of Diversity Officers in Higher Education (NADOHE). From my observation of over 300 attendees, I am the only Asian American among a majority of Blacks/African Americans, a handful of Latin@s, a handful of Whites, and a few Native Americans. The symbolism of this representation prompted me to wonder, "Are we ready for an Asian American Chief Diversity Officer?" If we consider the complex pieces of this question and work through the paths to which it could leads us, I believe we can have a transformative dialogue that will guide us in our journeys to unhooking from Whiteness.

Joy L. Lei, Ph.D.
Chief Diversity and Inclusivity Officer,
University of LaVerne
Spring 2013

ABOUT THE CONTRIBUTORS

René Antrop-González, Ph.D., Professor and Goizueta Chair at Dalton State College in Dalton Georgia where he teaches bilingual education courses. He also has experience teaching English as a second language and ESL at the elementary, high school, and college levels in Puerto Rico and the United States. His research interests include African American and Latin@ sociology of education, urban school reform, and African American and Latin@ high achievers. Antrop-González received his M.Ed. in teaching of English as a second language at the Pontifical Catholic University of Puerto Rico and his Ph.D. in curriculum and instruction with an emphasis in bilingual education from the Pennsylvania State University. He is the author of *Schools as Radical Sanctuaries: Decolonizing Urban Education Through the Eyes of Youth of Color and Their Teachers.*

Dana Bickmore, Ph.D., is an Assistant Professor in the Educational Leadership Program at Louisiana State University where her work involves the development of aspiring and practicing principals in urban and diverse schools. Dr. Bickmore also spent 28 years in public schools where she served as a teacher, assistant principal, principal, and district director of professional development. Her research interests include principal leadership in charter schools, the professional development of practicing principals, and the principal's role in induction, with publications appearing in national and international journals, such as the *Journal of School Leadership, Teaching and Teacher Education*, and the *International Journal of Educational Leadership Preparation.*

Steven T. Bickmore, Ph.D., is an Assistant Professor of English Education with a joint appointment in the School of Education and the English Department at Louisiana State University in Baton Rouge. He is also a co-editor of *The ALAN Review*, a journal about the teaching and research of young adult literature. His research interests include the induction and mentoring of novice teachers and how pre-service and novice English teachers negotiate the teaching of literature using young adult literature, especially around the issues of race, class, and gender. He taught high school English for 25 years in the suburbs of Salt Lake City, Utah.

Kenneth Fasching-Varner, Ph.D., is the Shirley B. Barton Assistant Professor of Elementary Education and Foundations at Louisiana State University in Baton Rouge, Louisiana. Fasching-Varner's research centers on Critical Race Theory with considerations of White racial identity development, culturally relevant pedagogy, and considerations of equity and diversity in a variety of educational settings including physical and virtual PreK-12 and higher education contexts.

C. Hayes and N.D. Hartlep (Eds.), Unhooking from Whiteness:
The Key to Dismantling Racism in the United States, 137–139.
© *2013 Sense Publishers. All Rights Reserved.*

Nicholas D. Hartlep, Ph.D., is an Assistant Professor of Educational Foundations at Illinois State University. He is the author of *Going Public: Critical Race Theory and Issues of Social Justice* (Tate Publishing, 2010), *The Model Minority Stereotype: Demystifying Asian American Success* (Information Age Publishing, 2013), and *The Model Minority Stereotype Reader: Critical and Challenging Readings for the 21st Century* (Cognella Academic Publishing, 2013). His most recent publication, "The Model Minority? Stereotypes of Asian American Students May Hurt More Than They Help" appears in *Diverse: Issues in Higher Education*. Hartlep feels that one critical component to the task of demystifying the Asian American model minority stereotype is to improve the dissemination of scholarly work on this insidious myth. He recently launched "The Model Minority Stereotype Project" (MMSP) (http://my.ilstu.edu/blogs/ndhartl/). The mission of the MMSP is focused on this aspect of access.

Cleveland Hayes, Ph.D., is an Associate Professor of Education in the College of Education and Organizational Leadership at the University of La Verne. At the University he teaches secondary methods, science methods for elementary teachers, and research methods. His research interests include culturally responsive teaching, history of Black education, Critical Race and Whiteness Theories in Education, and Latin@ students and teachers. His research can be found in *Power and Education, Democracy and Education*, and *International Journal of Qualitative Studies in Education*.

Brenda Juárez, Ph.D., is a former elementary public and private school teacher. Dr. Juárez has taught multicultural teacher education and social foundations courses in the Western United States and in the American Deep South. She now teaches in the Social Justice Education program at the University of Massachusetts, Amherst. Her research interests focus on documenting the teaching practices and perspectives of exemplary Black teachers of Black students in the US South and on examining ways regional geographies of opportunity and history influence the gaps in educational outcomes and experiences of African American learners and students from other historically disenfranchised social groups. Dr. Juárez has published on topics of Spanish-English dual language education programs in public schools, social justice and Whiteness in U.S. teacher education, the role of culture in successful teaching for Black students, and the transracial adoption of Black children by White parents. Her work has appeared in *The Journal of Black Studies; Democracy and Education;* and *The Journal of Race Ethnicity and Education*. She is co-author of *White Parents, Black Children: Understanding Adoption and Race* published in 2011 by Rowman & Littlefield.

Joy L. Lei, Ph.D., is Chief Diversity and Inclusivity Officer at the University of La Verne. Prior to this position, she was Assistant Campus Diversity Officer at the University of California, Santa Cruz, a program assistant at Facing History and Ourselves and an Assistant Professor at Vassar College. She co-edited *Global Constructions of Multicultural Education: Theories and Realities* with Carl A. Grant, which was published in 2001 by Lawrence Erlbaum and received the Multicultural Book Award from the National Association for Multicultural Education in 2002.

Karla Martin, Ph.D., is a member of the Poarch Band of Creek Indians. She is an Assistant Professor in the Department of Educational Administration and Foundations at Illinois State University. Her lifelong work is with the Poarch Creek community in the areas of education, history, and identity. She is currently on leave from Illinois State University as a postdoctoral fellow at Arizona State University.

Rosa Mazurett-Boyle, Ed.D., is a veteran K-12 teacher in the Rochester City School District where she works for the Dept. of World Languages. Her current research interests include Critical Race Mothering and Funds of Knowledge on teaching and learning. Dr. Mazurett-Boyle delivers workshops using Action Research methodology to educators seeking to understand real classroom issues. In the past two years she has led several initiatives to create culturally responsive curricula for the unique needs of urban World Language learners and heritage language students.

Rema Reynolds, Ph.D., is an Associate Professor in Azusa Pacific University's School Counseling and School Psychology Department. Dr. Reynolds also teaches Global Leadership classes abroad and undergraduate courses at UCLA. Having done most everything in schools from cleaning to leading, Dr. Reynolds is a consummate educator. Dr. Reynolds' research examines issues of parent engagement as they relate to Black families and student achievement, instructional strategies educators employ to honor and incorporate literacies students bring to the classroom, cultural competencies counselors and school counselors acquire through their respective preparatory programs, and the roles of school administrators in community and civic development. Her past articles and forthcoming books focus on engaging underrepresented parents in schools and provide practical guides and strategies for parents and school officials.

Margaret-Mary Sulentic Dowell, Ph.D., is an Associate Professor of Literacy and Urban Education at Louisiana State University, in Baton Rouge, Louisiana. Sulentic Dowell's research is focused on literacy in urban settings, specifically the complexities of literacy leadership, providing access to literature, and service-learning as a pathway to prepare pre-service teachers to teach reading authentically in urban environs. Sulentic Dowell is editor of *The E-Journal of Literacy and Social Responsibility*.

Matthew Witt, Ph.D., is associate professor of public administration at the University of La Verne. He is Professor published extensively in leading academic journals on matters of race and racism in the American institutional context. He is a frequent guest on the Progressive Talk Radio Network and expert panelist for Consensus 9/11: The 9/11 Best Evidence Panel. He is co-editor of a recently published collection of critical essays, *State Crimes Against Democracy: Political Forensics in Public Affairs* (Palgrave-MacMillan, 2013).

139

NAME INDEX

Names in the Name Index represent citation references. Biographical or autoethnographic accounts are included in the Subject Index.

SUBJECT INDEX

Names for biographical or autoethnographic accounts are included in the Subject Index. Names in the Name Index represent citation references.

CPSIA information can be obtained
at www.ICGtesting.com
Printed in the USA
BVOW06s2117171117
500675BV00009B/268/P